The Spiritual Society

THE
Spiritual
S●ciety

What Lurks beyond Postmodernism?

FREDERIC W. BAUE

CROSSWAY BOOKS • WHEATON, ILLINOIS

A DIVISION OF GOOD NEWS PUBLISHERS

Cover design: David LaPlaca

First printing, 2001

Printed in the United States of America

Scripture taken from the *Holy Bible: New International Version*, © 1973, 1978, 1984 by International Bible Society. Used by permission of Zondervan Publishing House. All rights reserved.

The "NIV" and "New International Version" trademarks are registered in the United States Patent and Trademark Office by International Bible Society. Use of either trademark requires the permission of International Bible Society.

Excerpt from *"Disjecta Membra"* is from *Black Zodiac* by Charles Wright. Copyright © 1997 by Charles Wright. Reprinted by permission of Farrar, Strauss and Giroux, LLC.

Excerpt of five lines from "Celestial Music" is from *Ararat* by Louise Glück. Copyright © 1990 by Louise Glück. Reprinted by permission of HarperCollins Publishers, Inc.

Excerpt from "Prophecy" is from *The One Day*. Copyright © 1988 by Donald Hall. Reprinted by permission of Ticknor & Fields/Houghton Mifflin Company. All rights reserved.

Excerpt from "The White Pilgrim: Old Christian Cemetery," copyright © 1995 by Brigit Pegeen Kelly is reprinted from *Song*, poems by Brigit Pegeen Kelly, with the permission of BOA Editions, Ltd.

Illustration of Thomas Merton copyright © by Robert Lentz, used courtesy of Trinity Stores, P.O. Box 44944, Eden Prairie, Minn., 55344 (800) 699-4482, www.trinitystores.com.

Library of Congress Cataloging-in-Publication Data
Baue, Frederic W., 1946-
    The spiritual society : what lurks beyond postmodernism? / Frederic W. Baue.
        p.   cm.
    Includes bibliographical references and index.
    ISBN 1-58134-253-5 (pbk. : alk. paper)
    1. Christianity and culture. I. Title.
BR115.C8 B385   2001
261—dc21   2001003248
                                                                              CIP

15	14	13	12	11	10	09	08	07	06	05	04	03	02	01
15	14	13	12	11	10	9	8	7	6	5	4	3	2	1

To my wife, Jean,
and my children—
Frederic, Michael, and Katherine

To my father,
who loves history while
looking forward to a future with Christ,

and to my mother,
who is in that living future now

10.14

Contents

Preface

It was a slow afternoon at the office of Trinity Lutheran Church, Rochester, Minnesota—one of those stretches you get now and then in parish ministry when all the hospital visits have been made and the sermon is in the can and you have to face sorting through that pile of papers that has been stacking up on your desk for weeks. Anything but that! So I drifted down to the church library to poke through a box of books that Mildred Beilke had brought in. Not that I had much hope of finding anything tasty. You know how church libraries are— kind of like a refrigerator full of nothing but leftovers, mostly moldy old stuff that someone less thrifty would pitch. But I rummaged around through the usual outdated *Reader's Digests* and castoff books and then came across an intriguing title: *The Crisis of Our Age*.

I'd been interested in such topics for some time, collecting books on Christianity and culture and attending lectures by Dr. Francis A. Schaeffer—I'd been a student at Swiss L'Abri a few years before— whenever he was in town for cancer treatment at the Mayo Clinic. Schaeffer, like me, was basically a pastor with a wider field of intellectual interests, and we'd get together from time to time and talk about change in civilization, movements in the arts, how and why they happened . . . that sort of thing. When the table of contents of the book in my hand indicated a work about just such things, I picked it up, took it back to my office, closed the door, and lit my pipe. And so, by happy accident, I was introduced to the thought of Pitirim A. Sorokin, a man one contemporary scholar called "a neglected genius."

Sorokin's analysis of cultural change was broader and deeper— and more prophetic—than anything I had yet encountered. His work, along with independent reading in theology and literature, began to unlock for me an understanding of why the twentieth century had been so turbulent and where our culture might be headed next. In the course of time I began to discuss these ideas with friends—including Professor Gene Edward Veith who encouraged me to write this book. Now I have even more clutter on my desk!

Nonetheless I wish to take this opportunity to thank Professor Veith for his encouragement and the editors at Crossway for giving me the opportunity to present these thoughts to the reading public. Along the way I was given valuable opportunities to speak on this topic in forums where perceptive and consecrated brothers and sisters in Christ raised points and asked questions that helped sharpen the argument. So let me express my appreciation to the faculty and students of Concordia Theological Seminary, St. Catherine's, Ontario—especially Professor John Stephenson—for the privilege of letting me deliver the 1999 Lutheran Life Lectures (Lutheran Life is a fraternal benefit society [insurance company] in Canada and generously sponsors the annual lecture series); to the Lutheran Church-Missouri Synod Michigan District 1999 pastor's conference; and to the Lutherans For Life Board of Directors 2000 retreat at the Benedictine Retreat Center, Schuyler, Nebraska (Lutherans For Life is a Christian pro-life organization [not an insurance company] in America).

Let me here plainly state my bias in favor of Lutheran theology. Indeed, I am bound to it by sacred ordination vows. I will be very thankful to anyone who can show me from Scripture where I may be in error. But I do have a theology. This may put me at odds in certain places with readers who adhere to Reformed or Arminian or Roman Catholic or Eastern Orthodox doctrine. I pray that the resulting dialogue will be a friendly one . . . and also that the binding will hold up in the event someone flings the book against the wall.

Colleagues in ministry reviewed earlier drafts of this manuscript and gave helpful insight and comments. Among these are the Reverend Doctors Philip H. Lochhaas, former director of the LCMS

Commission on [Religious] Organizations; Wilbert H. Rosin, past president of Concordia College, Milwaukee; Christopher W. Mitchell, editor of the Concordia Commentary Series; John F. Johnson, president of Concordia Seminary, St. Louis; Robert L. Rosin, chairman of the Department of Historical Theology at Concordia Seminary; Ronald R. Feuerhahn, professor of Historical Theology at Concordia Seminary; and Dean O. Wenthe, president of Concordia Theological Seminary, Ft. Wayne. (Non-Lutheran readers may be puzzled by the homogenous nomenclature; it comes from the *Concordia*, or *The Book of Concord* [1580], a compendium of Lutheran confessions, or doctrinal statements. Which explains why all us Lutherans think alike, or at least give everything the same name, which I guess is the next best thing.)

Finally, let me utter most heartfelt thanks to my dear wife, Jean, and my children, Rick, Mike, and Kate, for their patience during the long process of writing this book. Now it is done. Who knows, maybe a copy will end up in somebody's church library . . .

St. Bartholomew
2000

Introduction

The German director Fritz Lang, in his classic silent film, *Metropolis* (1926), depicts a technological utopia. Its alabaster city features flying machines, gee-whiz appliances, and a society that runs as smoothly as a well-oiled Teutonic machine. Everything is guided by reason, cool and sublime, even though the proletariat is oppressed. There is a labor uprising, but ultimately the opposing sides shake hands (literally) and the futuristic metropolis continues.

Trouble is, Lang's modernist cinematic vision, even in 1926, was already out-of-date. He depicted a worldly, nineteenth-century ideal, one in which mankind, ever more rapidly evolving through eugenics while exercising benign control over nature and building a perfected urban environment, finally arrived at a kind of secular New Jerusalem. Never mind that the idea of human progress is unique to the Christian West. As in Marx, so in this film and others like it, the theological undercurrents—both true and false—are sublimated and filtered through the mind of an industrial-revolution optimist.

Such a persistent utopian vision energized preachers, politicians, and the populace for generations. Indeed, it continues to do so. But even at the dawn of the twentieth century it was beginning to dim and splinter like a dark kaleidoscope. Voices of doubt about progress had begun to sound in the mid- to late-nineteenth century with authors like Matthew Arnold and Mark Twain. Then industrial Europe produced mechanized killing on an unimaginably horrifying scale in the Great War of 1914-1918. This cultural quake thrust a fault line through twentieth-century poetry—indeed, through all of the arts—and a note of anguish set in that never went away. The futuristic films of the late twentieth century became dark and apocalyptic, full of ruined cities and ragged people driven by lust and hunger: *Mad Max, Demolition Man, Waterworld* . . . the list goes on. So the artist's view of his culture was far more pessimistic in the twentieth century than it had been a hundred years before. It is this negative, secular worldview that most of us have grown up with. We call it Postmodernism.

Yet now at the dawn of the twenty-first century and the third millennium, that vision in turn seems outdated as a global economy rolls along in the wake of the computer revolution and yet another big shift in the arts begins to be felt. As has often been true in the past, cultural change registers first in the arts, and there among the poets before others. There are practical reasons for this. It just takes longer to write a novel or compose a symphony, and the economic machinery to produce those works of art is more complicated. A poem, by contrast, can be written in the morning, sold on the street in the afternoon, and read aloud that same evening. A change in the poet's worldview is felt immediately by the public. And the newest poetry in America today is beginning to register a change.

Analyzing cultural change is harder today than it used to be. A medieval peasant knew what the future held: more of the same. He lived in a static society; things didn't change much from generation to generation. So a futurist in the year 1000 would have been on firm ground in predicting a growing influence for the church of Rome and the continued development of a feudal economy. But for us today, change hurtles forward at a dizzying pace, and confident predictions are daily proven wrong. Those who predicted a coming utopia were both right and wrong. Things are better than they were in terms of health care, technology, and economic opportunity. At the same time, cities are unsafe, crime is rampant, and children are killing children while kids are having kids. "If present trends continue . . ." they begin. But the trends never seem to continue much beyond the present. Add to this the ever-vexing problem of periodization. When did the Modern Period begin? Some say the sixteenth century, others the seventeenth, still others with the French Revolution of 1789. The challenge is to find the simplicity in history—the patterns and trends and movements—without ignoring its complexity. *Caveat auctor*—let he who takes pen in hand to address these issues beware.

Yet there are ways in which a responsible Christian thinker can work through these problems without falling into comic-book scenarios. While the details are often in dispute, the basics of eschatology—the Bible's teaching on the future—are evident to all: We confess in the Apostles' Creed that we believe in the resurrected Christ who ascended into heaven and sits at the right hand of God, from whence He shall come to judge the living and the dead. In addition, our churchly intellectuals like Francis A. Schaeffer, Herbert Schlossberg, and Gene Edward Veith have applied their God-given minds to the subject of cultural analysis. So with study we can gain an understanding of where we have come from, where we are, and where we are going—all in Christ who is the same yesterday, today, and forever.

Consider it axiomatic that when church leaders finally catch on to a trend, it's over. Most of our people, both lay and clergy, are not involved enough in the arts to really know what's going on. The Counterculture movement of the Sixties ended at Kent State; yet trendy campus pastors were still doing bad folk masses with out-of-tune guitars way into the Seventies and Eighties. So it is today with Postmodernism. The buzzword is on everyone's lips in church circles, while in university English departments where the whole Pomo (Postmodern) thing began, other theories like New Historicism have taken over. I contend that Postmodernism is now fading away and is rapidly being supplanted by other cultural forces.

To learn what those forces may be, how they will influence our lives as Christians, and what we should do in response to them, I will sketch a picture of the past, take a snapshot of the present, and then draw a simple line into the future, connecting the dots of cultural trends. Those trends are already apparent to those who have ears to hear what our poets are trying to teach us.

Chapter One gives a Christian perspective on understanding the times, focusing especially on the dynamic of the Gospel of Jesus Christ as an agent of cultural change. Chapter Two reviews some secular philosophers of history and develops a philosophical framework for understanding cultural dynamics, drawing particularly upon the work of sociologist Pitirim A. Sorokin. Chapter Three begins to apply that framework to our Western civilization from the earliest times, especially as seen in the work of major poets. Chapter Four examines the early church in some detail, especially the forces against the Gospel that arose from within. Chapter Five treats Islam, one of the greatest early religious threats to the Christian faith. Chapter Six discusses the Middle Ages and shows how the Gospel continued its activity during that time. Chapter Seven examines the beginnings of the Modern Period and looks at the development of Postmodernism. Chapter Eight is about "the Therian Age," my term for an emerging major trend in our culture—a dominant religious mode that is hostile to Christianity. Chapter Nine concludes the book with a word about what the Church should do in response to the major cultural change that is coming upon us. Through all of this it will be seen that we have a gracious God who sustains His people in times of trouble, not because we deserve it, but because of the saving death and resurrection of His Son, our Lord and Savior Jesus Christ.

1

Understanding the Times

The poet David would have had sympathy for us. He, too, lived in a critical period, a time of turmoil and uncertainty, a time of transition between two contending cultural forces, one—that of Saul, with its compromising sympathy for Canaanite religion—waning, the other—that of David, with its pure strain of Hebrew discipleship—gathering strength. Among those who came to David at Hebron were "men of Issachar, who understood the times and knew what Israel should do" (1 Chronicles 12:32). The situation was critical. Saul's regime, so accommodating to established cultural influences, had fallen. David, long ago anointed king, was now ready to come into his kingdom. He needed leadership. He needed men who could read the signs of the times, give sound advice, and ascertain the wisest course of action. David got the direction he needed and ascended to the throne of Israel. We need men and women like that now, sanctified thinkers and artists who can discern cultural trends in the world and help formulate an appropriate response by the Church today.

Evangelism

Key to an understanding of history must be an awareness of the centrality of evangelism. Our Lord indicated as much when He said,

"Upon this rock [the confession that Jesus is the Christ] I will build my church; and the gates of hell shall not prevail against it" (Matthew 16:18, KJV). That is to say, the proclamation of justification by grace through faith in Jesus Christ is the responsibility of the Church and will be accomplished with the help of the Lord of the Church. Beginning at Jerusalem, then spreading to Judea and Samaria, and from thence to all the ends of the earth, the Church will carry this message of salvation to all people, shaping history as it goes.

The devil will oppose this work of God; it is an invasion of his miserable kingdom of darkness. He will foment persecution from without and heresy from within. But he will not prevail. He will walk about like a roaring lion, devour some, draw many away from the faith, and impede the progress of the Gospel. But he will not succeed. Jesus promised that He Himself would build His Church.

How can this be accomplished, given the weakness and frailty of all-too-human disciples? Herein lies a mystery—one more paradox in a Church where the last are first—weakness overcomes power. As Jesus prepared for His passion He said, "Now is the time for judgment on this world; now the prince of this world will be driven out" (John 12:31). In the weakness of His death, He destroyed sin, death, and the power of the devil. This action is described symbolically in the last book of the Bible: "He [Christ] seized the dragon, that ancient serpent, who is the devil, or Satan, and bound him for a thousand years" (Revelation 20:2). In other words, the Lord limited the power of Satan to deceive the nations so that the Gospel could be proclaimed all over the world for a long period of time. That's the simplest explanation of this verse. It should be obvious that if the devil had his way, the Gospel would be preached nowhere; there would be no Church, no pastors, no faith, no Sacraments. But the impossible has happened. Christian people—all their faults notwithstanding—have in fact spread the saving Gospel of Jesus Christ all over the world.

Wherever the Gospel has been preached, people have responded to its message of salvation, and congregations have been formed. With the growth of the Church, cities have been transformed by its influence—that is to say, by the cumulative influence of individual Christian men and women being involved in the secular affairs of the city and bringing to bear on its problems the mind of Christ. City by city, nations and civilizations have likewise been transformed. As the Roman senate filled up with Christian leaders, it passed laws against abortion and infanticide. Something like this seems to have been the purport of Jesus' parable about the mustard seed: "[The kingdom of God] is like a mustard seed, which a man took and planted in his garden. It grew and became a tree, and the birds of the air perched in its branches" (Luke 13:19). Conservative interpreters read this as follows: The tree is the kingdom of God. It starts small and becomes large. The birds come and go; they are people of the world not attached to the kingdom directly. The branches are the fringe benefits of the Church to a nation that allows it to flourish. Included are those secondary institutions created by or influenced by the Church, such as the arts, education, law, government, business, medicine, and so forth. These ultimately provide benefits even to people who do not belong to the Church. Millions today benefit from a university education, little realizing that the institution was invented by the Church.

Conversely, civilizations that reject the Gospel suffer practical consequences. It comes as a shock but ultimately no surprise that the U.S. Senate, where Christian influence has long been in eclipse, would refuse to pass laws against abortion and infanticide that have been handed up to it by the House of Representatives. Thus the lives of the unborn and newborn remain unprotected in America, and the first unalienable right is set aside in favor of "choice."

For these reasons I maintain that the Gospel of Jesus Christ is the key to history. Western civilization is largely a by-product of the Gospel. Its rise and its fall are intensely interesting to us, for it is *our* civilization, and our immediate livelihood and well-being depend upon its stability. But what is of ultimate importance is the kingdom of God—that is, the Church, that divine institution that is in the world

but not of the world, and through which God calls people to repentance and saves them for everlasting life.

As the progress of the Gospel influences civilization, the decay of
a civilization can impede the progress of the Gospel. Someone once
compared history to the scaffolding around Noah's ark. With such a
bewildering profusion of boards and ladders, you can hardly make out
what's being built behind it. This is how we often look at the institutions of society—government, education, law, economics—the temporal structures that surround and support the Church and within
which its planks are fitly joined together. We see it all, and sometimes
the scaffolding seems more solid and impressive than the construction
project itself with all of its delays, cost overruns, staff shortages, and
mistakes that have to be corrected. Yet the work goes on from generation to generation, and one Noah after another arises to be a preacher
of righteousness, proclaiming the Word of the Gospel by which the
ship is being built. One by one and two by two, people are gathered
in and find sanctuary. Finally the rain comes down, the streams rise,
the winds blow and beat against the scaffolding, and it washes away
while the ark of salvation, the Church of Jesus Christ, floats away on
baptismal waters to a new world of everlasting bliss. For the first
world, it was the *eschaton*, the end of all things. And so will it be for
us in our world.

Grace and Faith

Somehow the Bible has a way of connecting water with acts of salvation and damnation, with blessing and curse. Adam and Eve drank
from a river in the Garden of Eden. Noah and his family "were saved
through water" while a sinful world perished (1 Peter 3:20). Moses
led the people of Israel through the Red Sea—the same sea that
destroyed Pharaoh's army. Joshua led the Israelites through the parted
waters of the Jordan River. Naaman found healing from leprosy in the
simple act of bathing. John came preaching a Baptism unto repen-

tance. Dead works were to be drowned in the water. Jesus said that to be saved, we must be born again of water and the Spirit. Indeed, He described Himself as living water (John 4:10). At the very end of the Bible we see the river of the water of life, flowing from the throne of God (Revelation 22:17).

While some may dispute whether all of these passages refer to Baptism, one area of universal agreement is that "whoever believes and is baptized will be saved" (Mark 16:16). Faith is essential for salvation. Jesus could die on the cross for the sins of the world a thousand times, but if nobody believed in Him, it wouldn't do anybody any good. No one would be saved, even though salvation had been won for them. Christ's death validates His last will and testament. You are his legitimate heir by adoption. It is faith that credits all the assets of Jesus Christ to your account. Faith is your signature on the check God issues from His treasury. Though on the cross Jesus died for all people in all places at all times, it is only by faith that you can say, "He died for *me*. He is *my* Savior." Not that faith is something you can produce by your own will or reason or emotions. No; even faith itself comes by grace. It is a gift of God, so that all credit for salvation goes to Him alone.

Along with faith, Baptism is considered important by all, regardless of disagreements on the outward form Baptism should take. Some argue for immersion, others sprinkling; some say adults only, others admit infants; some insist that it is a Sacrament, others that it is a divine ordinance but not a means of grace. Nevertheless, the importance of Baptism is unquestionably clear, since it is commanded by the Lord: "Therefore go and make disciples of all nations, baptizing them in the name of the Father and of the Son and of the Holy Spirit" (Matthew 28:19).

The case of the thief on the cross proves that under extreme circumstances one can be saved by faith alone without Baptism. Even so, this seems to be the exception that proves the rule, for the Bible frequently speaks of Baptism in connection with salvation. "Repent and be baptized, every one of you, in the name of Jesus Christ for the forgiveness of your sins. And you will receive the gift of the Holy Spirit. The promise is for you and your children and for all who are far off—for all whom the Lord our God will call" (Acts 2:38-39). Accordingly, the Church throughout the ages and down to the present has baptized those who have repented of their sins and confessed faith in Christ. All agree that Christ has commanded Baptism and that under normal circumstances a Christian should be baptized.

Baptism

Connecting with Noah's Flood in this regard, it may be helpful to consider the eschatological dimension of Baptism. St. Paul writes, "Don't you know that all of us who were baptized into Christ Jesus were baptized into his death? We were therefore buried with him through baptism into death in order that, just as Christ was raised from the dead through the glory of the Father, we too may live a new life" (Romans 6:3-4). Water gives life and takes it away. The Flood meant salvation for Noah, destruction for the first world. In the same way, the water of Baptism works in two ways. It kills your Old Adam; it brings your New Man to life. It is an individual *eschaton* through water.

Christ died on the cross. There was His end. Those who believe and are baptized are joined with Him in His death. His end becomes our end. In His death, all of our sins are washed away, and all the debts we owed to God are now paid. In Christ we are now dead to sin, just as a corpse in a coffin is impervious to temptation.

Christ rose again from the dead. There was His new beginning. Those who believe and are baptized are joined with Him in His resurrection. His new beginning becomes our new beginning. In His resurrection, we now stand before God justified, declared innocent in His eternal court of law. We are now given the Holy Spirit and filled with power for living a new life. Old things are passed away; all has become new.

In other words, what is true of faith is true of Baptism. Both go together to take what Christ has done and make it your own. In these things the benefits of Christ's holy, innocent death and resurrection are made yours. When Scripture says in one place that a man is saved by grace through faith and in another that he who believes and is baptized shall be saved, it is saying the same thing.

Many a new convert to Christ can testify what a life-changing experience this is. Sometimes it is sudden and dramatic, sometimes slow and gradual, but always there is a fundamental change that takes place in the person who believes and is baptized. It is as if he had died to the old life and entered into a whole new world full of grace and peace and joy in Christ. Old things have passed away; all has become new. The flood waters have rampaged through his world, and he has experienced both damnation and salvation. For him as an individual it *is* the end of the world, it *is* the coming of Christ.

Hence the cheerful resignation with which the faithful in all generations have faced the cross, persecution, adversity, and mere temporal death. With all their hearts and all their minds and all their strength they are focused not on the things of this world but on the world that is unseen, above, and coming. It has been well said that everybody wants to go to heaven, but nobody wants to have to die to get there. For true believers in Christ, though, there is a very deep dimension of life in which the future lies in the past. He who is to come *has* come into their hearts. By faith in Christ and baptism into Christ, the struggle of death has been eased, the sting salved, the sword blunted. For the individual Christian who dies, the end has come.

What this does is place a *terminus ad quem* upon the history of each individual. A man lives once. There never was anyone exactly like him, nor will there ever be again. His story is unique, his life like none other. Because it has an end, it has a beginning and a middle. Each man's life is a little history and a piece of the whole. Each man knows at some level, deep or shallow, that he will face his end one day. He may fight it, but in the end he will die. And this knowledge of the end will inevitably, in some way, have an influence on his activities today.

At some point a man will do something in the present that gives symbolic recognition to death that may seem a long way off but is still on the track like a slow train coming. He will take out an insurance policy for the benefit of his survivors. He will make out a will for the orderly disposition of his worldly goods. He may start going back to church. Or on the other hand he may get a divorce, grow a ponytail, buy a Harley, and shack up with some young floozy. Whatever he does, he is in some way tipping his hat to the grim reaper. The future determines the present.

For those who are being saved, the future meets the present on a daily basis. As Paul says, "I die every day" (1 Corinthians 15:31). That is, in Christ, repentance is not just a one-time experience; it is something that is everyday and ongoing. The Old Adam keeps struggling for control, the flesh lusting against the Spirit. We often sin, stumble, and fall. Yet we repent just as often, beg God for mercy, and experience the blessed forgiveness of Christ many times a day and receive power to live a new life. On the whole, we are radically different than we were before we believed; but the struggle never ceases until it is resolved in death and we enter everlasting life. For the present, death and life wrestle. This is the action of Baptism in the Christian's daily life. The water swirls and flows and cascades with currents and undertows like a mighty flood. But now at the end of the day we find Adam drowned and Christ victorious, death swallowed up by life.

This is why in traditional denominations where the ancient liturgy has been kept, the faithful often make the sign of the cross at significant points in the service as well as every morning for daily personal devotions. It is a remembrance of Baptism, when the minister first made the sign of the holy cross over the heart of the penitent as a sign that he had been redeemed by Christ the crucified. The curse was upon Jesus, the blessing upon us. The Law was meted out to Him, the Gospel delivered to us. For Him, damnation; for us, salvation. In the water of Baptism God kills and makes alive. In this water, for each man on every day of his life, it is the end of the old world and the beginning of the new.

Last Things

In addition to the individual, there is also a corporate eschatology that occupies the minds of believers and theologians. As with Baptism, much controversy has surrounded this doctrine of Last Things—perhaps an indication of its importance. There are premillennialists and postmillennialists and amillennialists, all contending for their interpretations; and within the premillennialist camp there are pre-tribbers and mid-tribbers and post-tribbers, complicating matters even further. Opinions are often entrenched. All this notwithstanding, there are surprisingly large areas of common agreement among us who confess Jesus Christ.

In the Apostles' Creed we declare that we believe in Jesus Christ who "ascended into heaven," and "from thence He shall come to judge the living and the dead." According to the faith that has been believed everywhere by everyone, we believe in "the resurrection of the body, and the life everlasting." That is the irreducible minimum, the fundamental confidence we all share that at some future day, known only to God, Jesus Christ will return to this earth to judge all people, raising all bodies from their graves, sending the unjust into eternal perdition and the righteous into the eternal joy of heaven.

One might say that the Second Coming has already taken place in the Resurrection of Jesus Christ. In a sense, it has. That is, in a proleptic or anticipatory sense. Christ's resurrection was a once-and-for-all event, never to be repeated. He was put to death for our sins and raised again for our justification. Once killed and once raised, he never has to go through it again. But in His resurrection is contained the seed, the potential, of the end of the world. The event has a finality about it—the defeat of all evil, the vanquishing of the grave, the triumph over Satan. His individual resurrection looks forward to the resurrection of all flesh that He promised before the Ascension. And inasmuch as the Resurrection is a proleptic event, Christians today, as throughout all ages, live in victory even while under the cross.

Another aspect of realized eschatology is in the Lord's Supper, often called Holy Communion. It purports to bring us into communion with God, who dines only with His friends. In liturgical churches, just before the Communion the minister says in the *Sanctus*, "With angels and archangels and with all the company of heaven we laud and magnify Thy Glorious Name." The idea is that we are ushered into the presence of God in this simple but holy meal Christ gave us, and that we are there together with everyone else who stands in the presence of God in heaven, all saints and all angels. It is as if we were proleptically sent forward in time to the marriage supper of the Lamb.

What this does is place a *terminus ad quem* upon history. The Christian knows that all things ultimately conspire to this end: the Second Coming of Jesus Christ. God works all things for the ultimate good, for the redemption of His people. He moves men and nations and events forward in His own mysterious way toward the final day of destiny. Every dramatic occurrence, every catastrophe—and somehow they seem to come in clusters, like the increasingly frequent and intense contractions of a woman in labor—moves history forward toward its final goal. Someday the world will end. Someday all the loose threads of human events will come together in a final conflict between good and evil. Someday the trumpet will sound. History in this context can be said to be a combination of two dynamics. It is not only a product of past causes that push from behind, as many have observed; it is also and perhaps ultimately the product of a future event that draws it forward. The future determines the present.

So if the Gospel is the key to history in an ongoing sense, it is also the key to history in a final sense. The death and resurrection of Christ—*the* Gospel event—turned over the hourglass of time. The preaching of the Gospel in the world is a sign of the coming end. And when we celebrate Holy Communion—what St. Augustine called "the visible Word"—we "proclaim the Lord's death until he comes" (1 Corinthians 11:26). The age of grace and the end times are one and the same.

Jesus said, "This gospel of the kingdom will be preached in the whole world as a testimony to all nations, and then the end will come" (Matthew 24:14). Some missionary groups have calculated the number of languages in the world that do not yet have a New Testament, with the implication that as soon as they get the Gospel translated into every tongue and preach a sermon in it, Christ will return. While their efforts are praiseworthy, it is doubtful that God is bound by such a mechanical imperative.

Nevertheless, it may be that missionaries—those hardy and adventurous men and women who hazard their bodies to deliver the Gospel to the darkened corners of this world (including America, as denominational mission analysts are now recognizing)—stand in our midst like an indicator species. Their progress, or lack thereof, may be important to understanding the ebb and flow of human events. Years ago, when I was a student at Concordia Seminary, St. Louis, I asked now-sainted Professor Martin Scharlemann about Jesus' saying concerning the fig tree: "As soon as its twigs get tender and its leaves come out, you know that summer is near" (Matthew 24:32-33). He said that in his opinion we need to keep our eye on the missionaries; if the day ever comes when they can no longer do their work and their host countries begin to expel them, look up.

Expectation

What this sets up in the minds of believers is an expectation of Christ's return. Our minds on things above, we look to the sky in hope. From heaven our salvation draws near. Not just mine. Ours. All of us in the Church on earth, together with angels and archangels and all the company of heaven, cry out, "Come quickly, Lord Jesus!" This glorious appearing of Jesus Christ will bring an end to human history. All of history's pomp and vainglory, all of its power and riches—all will be overthrown in a moment, in the twinkling of an eye. The last will be first and the first last. The divine comedy will play out its final scene, and the curtain will come down upon human events, to the great laughter and applause of the saints whose groans and cries of anguish have gone up like fragrant incense to the throne of God throughout the whole long struggle of the age of grace.

Churchmen of every age have expected to see the fulfillment of the eschatological hope within their lifetimes. St. Paul thought so. St. Augustine thought so. Luther thought so. And with some justification, even though they were mistaken. In every age the dynamics of the end times have always been present. The Gospel has been preached. The Church has been under the cross. There have been signs in the heavens and upon the earth—eclipses and comets, floods and famines, wars and rumors of wars. We look at our own age and say, "Surely these are the last of the last days." Like our illustrious predecessors, we may be wrong. But what is certain is that one day, one generation will be right. Therefore all generations must be prepared, just as down the centuries every mother in Israel hoped to give birth to the Christ and so maintained an attitude of perpetual readiness.

Periods

New Testament writers used the word *kairos*, usually translated "age" or "epoch," to describe a long period of time marked by a signal, culminating historic event. This is certainly clear from Scripture and so can be held as a simple article of faith without delving into the complexities of dispensationalism. The Creation, the Fall, Noah's Flood, the Tower of Babel, the call of Abraham, the giving of the Law to Moses, the reign of King David, and the Babylonian Captivity certainly qualify as epochal events of the Old Testament. St. Matthew divides his genealogy into three periods: "fourteen generations in all from Abraham to David, fourteen from David to the exile to Babylon, and fourteen from the exile to the Christ" (1:17). And St. Paul says of the epoch that saw the fulfillment of the promise, "When the time had fully come, God sent his Son" (Galatians 4:4).

In the same way Jesus defines the end times as an age characterized by the proclaiming of salvation by faith in Christ and culminating in the Second Coming. "Go and make disciples of all nations, baptizing them in the name of the Father and of the Son and of the Holy Spirit, and teaching them to obey everything I have commanded you. And surely I am with you always, to the very end of the age" (Matthew 28:19-20). He warns against becoming preoccupied with eschatological speculation, saying that we should occupy ourselves with evangelism: "It is not for you to know the times or dates the Father has set by his own authority. But you will receive power when the Holy Spirit comes on you; and you will be my witnesses in Jerusalem, and in all Judea and Samaria, and to the ends of the earth" (Acts 1:7-8). With these clear Scriptures in mind, we see that while the Second Coming of Christ will be the culminating sign of the end, the preaching of the Gospel is the ongoing sign of the last days.

While so occupied, however, it is given to believers to have a certain general awareness of the times in which they live. In Matthew 24, Mark 13, and Luke 21, Jesus outlines the signs of the times to whet our appetite for the wedding supper of the Lamb: "Now learn this lesson from the fig tree: As soon as its twigs get tender and its leaves come out, you know that summer is near. Even so, when you see all these things, you know that it is near, right at the door" (Matthew 24:32-33). The majority of the people of this world will be preoccupied with worldly things and will be caught off guard by the Second Coming of Christ. Some wag even came up with a final headline for the *New York Times*, all in doomsday type: CHRIST RETURNS—STOCKS TUMBLE. Those who know Jesus will be ready. "But you, brothers, are not in darkness so that this day should surprise you like a thief" (1 Thessalonians 5:4). The faithful will be watching the signs of the times and exhorting one another to preparedness, evangelism, good works, and holy living.

Within this last age of the world, between the First and Second Coming, while signs of the approaching end are ongoing and the work of preaching goes forward, there are indications of smaller periods characterized by their own signal events. The beginning saw an emphasis on outreach to the Jews (Acts 1:8). This came to pass. Jesus said that the Gentiles would be converted (Acts 1:8). This came to pass. Christians expected that their religion would increase to great proportions (Matthew 13:31-33). This came to pass. It was a *kairos*. The time was right.

But Scripture also teaches that late in the last days there will be a change of atmosphere surrounding the Gospel. "Because of the increase of wickedness, the love of most will grow cold, but he who stands firm to the end will be saved" (Matthew 24:12-13). The expansion of the Church will slow down. "The Spirit clearly says that in later times some will abandon the faith" (1 Timothy 4:1). "That day shall not come, except there come a falling away first" (2 Thessalonians 2:3, KJV). The hand of God that held back Satan's attacks from the Church will be taken away, and "Satan will be released from his prison and will go out to deceive the nations in the four corners of the earth" (Revelation 20:7).

Something like this seems to have come to pass in our own time. The United Methodist Church, one of America's largest Protestant denominations, has shrunk by 30 percent since 1970—a loss of market share that would drive any business into the ground. Megachurches draw bigger and bigger crowds, while small congregations quietly slip away like old folks in a nursing home. One denominational executive was heard to remark that when the statistical reports of rapidly growing congregations using church growth methods are corrected for local demographics, the difference disappears. In other words, the church that is growing by 10 percent per year is located in a community that is growing by 10 percent or more per year.

Meanwhile the Mormons have exploded out of Utah and developed a savvy ad campaign that makes them look almost like a regular Christian denomination. Almost. Not that the mainline Protestant denominations are helping any with their espousal of doctrines that contradict the Scriptures, beginning with their adoption of a modernist theology that denies the inspiration of the Bible. Plus, New Age ideas are filtering into every level of religious thought, with erstwhile Christians holding views diametrically opposed to the faith, as any working pastor can tell you. And despite the considerable spiritual energy created in the past fifty years by Billy Graham Crusades, the Ecumenical Movement, the Charismatic Movement, Key '73, I Found It, the Jesus Freaks, *The Lutheran Hour*, the Liturgical Renewal, the Fellowship of Christian Athletes, Young Life, Campus Crusade, Navigators, Inter-Varsity, the Institute in Basic Youth Conflicts, L'Abri, contemporary Christian music, celebrity converts, televangelism, the Full Gospel Businessmen's Fellowship, Women's Aglow, the Church Growth movement, and Promise Keepers, the overall percentage of the population in church on Sunday—the one reliable statistical indicator of real religious activity in the nation—has remained constant at around 40 percent. In short, there's no revival going on. We're not in the next Great Awakening.

Regarding this falling away theologian John Stephenson says, "We live in the throes of a tragic intra-ecclesial defection from Christ which currently poses a massive threat to the integrity of His church as she subsists in a multiplicity of confessions and denominations. . . . Already two generations ago [Lutheran theologian Francis] Pieper was fully aware of the deep apostasy afflicting Christendom, being moved . . . to assert that history had in fact entered upon the 'little season' of Rev. 20:3" (3, 7). Can this be right? Today the Christian faith is persecuted but growing in Africa and Asia, while it has stagnated in America and shriveled in Europe.

Those who think about these things keep a close watch on the leaves of the fig tree, so to speak. They know that they cannot calculate the day and hour of Christ's return and so must keep watch on a daily basis, redeeming the time, for the days are evil. At the same time, like the men of Issachar, they make a responsible effort to understand the times in which they live and to know what the Church should do.

2

A Model of Historical Change

Secular thinkers have attempted to understand the times, albeit with limited success. This is not to argue that there is nothing of value produced by the secular mind. Far from it. God who created the world and all things in it is a loving heavenly Father and sends rain upon both the just and the unjust. He distributes natural gifts among the men and women of the human race, whether they are saved or not. Intellectual gifts are given to all kinds of people, Christian and non-Christian. Secular thinkers have recognized the brilliant work of the greatest Christian minds. Conversely, the Christian does well to glean wisdom from the best secular thinkers. Among the best-known philosophers of history are Karl Marx, Oswald Spengler, H. G. Wells, and Arnold Toynbee. Each in his own way peered into the mystery of major cultural change. Some were optimistic, others pessimistic. For our purposes, the most helpful model of historical change—and one that is more consistent with a Christian worldview—can be found in the work of Pitirim A. Sorokin.

Marx

Karl Marx (1818-1883) formulated a substitute kingdom of God in Communism. Deriving his ideas from the thought of Hegel, Marx outlined a theory of class struggle centered in dialectical materialism. Hegel had taught that ideas and political movements are ratified by a process of three steps (sometimes called "the Hegelian waltz"): thesis, antithesis, and synthesis. That is, a radical thinker will put forth a new idea (thesis), but traditional thinkers will immediately oppose it (antithesis). However, the force of the new idea will carry it forward, the opposition will begin to absorb and adopt some of its positions, and finally a new position will emerge, comprised of elements of the new and the old (synthesis).

Marx held that Communism or united labor was the new idea (thesis), opposing the entrenched powers of traditional capitalism (antithesis [the term *capitalism* was actually coined by Marx]), in which the means of production were controlled by the ruling class. Eventually government would wither away, and a worker's paradise would emerge, a classless society in which labor would control the means of production (synthesis).

In *The Communist Manifesto*, first published in Germany in 1848, Marx and his friend and co-revolutionary Friedrich Engels outline a totalizing philosophy of history based on the theory of class struggle: "In every historical epoch the prevailing mode of economic production and exchange, and the social organization necessarily following from it, form the basis upon which is built up, and from which alone can be explained, the political and intellectual history of that epoch; that, consequently, the whole history of mankind . . . has been a history of class struggles, contests between exploiting and exploited, ruling and oppressed classes; that the history of these class struggles forms a series of evolutions in which, nowadays, a stage has been reached where the exploited and oppressed class—the proletariat—cannot attain its emancipation from the sway of the exploiting and ruling class—the bourgeoisie—without at the same time, and once and for all, emancipating society at large from all exploitation, oppression, class distinctions and class struggles" (416).

The complaint here is that the bourgeoisie created progress

through industrialization, developed a world market, and brought "all nations, even the most barbarian, into civilization" (421). Civilization is inextricably tied to economic factors and built for the benefit of the middle and upper classes at the cost of the exploitation and oppression of the working class.

Marx doesn't seem to like progress and material comfort; he demonstrates a palpable nostalgia for primitive society. Nor is he happy about the fact that in the factories women can compete with men: "The less the skill and exertion of strength implied in manual labour—in other words, the more modern industry develops—the more is the labour of men superseded by that of women" (423). Not that Marx ever got out there and competed. With a doctorate from the University of Jena, Europe's most notorious diploma mill, Marx was content to theorize, providing little material comfort for his family. Had he lived long enough to see his ideas implemented, he could have gotten welfare for his wife and children, or more likely a comfortable academic sinecure for himself.

On a theoretical level, one can see the parallels between Marxism and Christian postmillennial eschatology. In this line of theological thought, the Church gradually penetrates every level of society and eventually creates a *thousand-year* reign of peace, justice, and prosperity, at the *end* of which Christ returns. Hence the term *postmillennial.* In other words, the kingdom of God is something we create by our own efforts with the help of God, creating a more perfect world and doing away with unjust things like class distinctions, racial prejudice, and the exploitation of labor. Perhaps this explains some of the appeal of Socialism to liberal thinkers in the Church. Fritz Mondale and Hillary Clinton, for example, both grew up Methodists— Mondale a minister's son. Among Catholics, the Maryknollers advocate a Socialist agenda, while some radical priests in Central America work for Marxist revolution. At the same time this line of theological and political thought can appeal to conservatives who want to reconstruct society along the lines of Old Testament law, saying, for example, that homosexuals should be stoned. Liberal or conservative, Postmillennialism is a real force in large segments of the wider Church.

Back in my coffeehouse days I overheard a conversation between two nationally-known folksingers. (The idea in those days was that the folksingers [who were all college-educated] were by means of protest songs going to foment the revolution of the working classes [who were all listening to Motown]). They delved deeply into Marxist theory. Later one fellow remarked about the other, "His history is perfect." That is, he understood that Marxism is essentially a philosophy of history and that all human events are to be comprehended in terms of the struggle between the proletariat and the bourgeoisie over the means of production. Not only human action but human thought: "Law, morality, religion are . . . so many bourgeois prejudices, behind which lurk in ambush just as many bourgeois interests" (424). Marx confidently predicted that the fall of the bourgeoisie and the "victory of the proletariat are equally inevitable" (425). The assumption of the Marxists is that history (like biology for the Darwinists) is on their side.

Let the reader judge the accuracy of these predictions. Nevertheless, many of Marx's theories have been implemented, and not only in Communist countries. Communism advocates abolition of the family, public education (as opposed to home schooling), and a women's movement, as well as income tax, nationalized banking, and a centralized communications media (427, 429). Obviously, all of these are well-established in America today, despite the fact that Communism has been rejected by most countries that have tried it. One might point out the exception of China, but experts such as Henry Rowold doubt whether *any* system of thought imported from the outside can have a lasting influence in the Middle Kingdom (with the possible exception of Christianity). Many have noted the continued influence of Marxism on Western political thought and its strength in university circles. But for our purposes here we simply note the broad sweep of the Communist view of history as an attempt to understand human events.

Spengler

The most pessimistic philosophy of history was set forth by Oswald Spengler (1880-1936) in his widely-read *Decline of the West* (1918, 1922). The title in German is *Untergang des Abendlandes*, which can be literally translated as "going under" or "sinking" of the "evening" or Western lands. Spengler held that Western civilization was coming to an end like Rome, never to rise again: "Each Culture has its own new possibilities of self-expression which arise, ripen, decay, and never return" (17). For example, according to Spengler the unique civilization of the ancient Greeks arose and flourished in its day. But it went into decline and decay, and now it is gone. Dead. Never to rise again. No sculptor works in the style of Praxiteles anymore. Likewise nothing remains of the medieval world. It rose, declined, and fell. Who today writes music in the style of Leonin?

Spengler, a teacher of mathematics, had actually completed work on the first volume of his philosophy of history before the outbreak of World War I. The war delayed publication until 1918. Spengler had accurately observed increasing opposition to traditional repositories of cultural values such as the nobility, the church, and the arts. He saw a rise of gross materialism in people's desire for sex, food, and entertainment (*panem et circenses*). "All these things," Spengler concluded, "betoken the definite closing down of the Culture and the opening of a quite new phase of human existence—anti-provincial, late, futureless, but nevertheless quite inevitable" (26).

In the post-war *ennui*, so well-known to readers of Hemingway and Fitzgerald and captured so poignantly in the musical *Cabaret*, the ideas that Spengler had worked out years earlier began to catch on. It certainly seemed that a great civilization was coming to an end. There was an apocalyptic feeling in the air. Spengler became widely read and powerfully influential. Look up the word *Spenglerian* in your dictionary. Subsequent thinkers had to respond to his thought.

Whether or not Spengler is widely read among Christians today, his judgment still remains over our world like a raven croaking doom from the naked branch of a dead tree. The idea of the impending collapse of Western civilization that gripped post-World War II Europe so powerfully has now taken hold in America. Like the undercoat of a painting that is unseen but determines the hue of everything on the surface, it may be that Spenglerian assumptions drive some Christians to give up on secular enterprises like politics and the arts and retreat to enclaves where they can live in peace in an alternative society based on Christian principles. Who can blame them? St. Benedict had the same idea when he founded the first monastery during the long and painful fall of Rome.

There are flaws in Spengler's concept. He fails to recognize that past cultures continue to influence the present to a greater or lesser degree through the words that originated in them and continue to be used today. Our contemporary speech is peppered with words and phrases that derive from Greek and Latin sources. Through the words come the ideas that continue to resonate like the inaudible overtones that give the piano its timbre and sonority. Many of the words that continue to shape our civilization derive from the Bible. With them comes a sprinkling of salt, the overall influence of Christianity that acts as a preservative in our cultural institutions. The idea of a charismatic leader, for example, comes from the New Testament Greek word *charisma*, or "gift," which in turns comes from *charis*, or "grace." In Christianity, God out of the fullness of His grace gives spiritual gifts to the members of His Church for the purpose of service and ministry. As the concept filters out of the Church and into society at large, the expectation arises that our political leaders will use their God-given abilities in a humble manner for the benefit of the people they serve. This kind of expectation of a leader is only possible in a (at least residually) Christian nation. Contrast this with the kind of merciless Oriental despots you find in the world like Nebuchadnezzar of old or Saddam Hussein and Mao Tse-tung in our day, who arise from cultures in which the Church has had no influence whatsoever. Like a citizen of Pompeii, Spengler fails to take into account the presence of the enormous volcano in whose shadow he lives—the Church, seemingly so dormant but liable to erupt when least expected, though not to destroy but to renew.

Wells

Unlike Spengler, H. G. (Herbert George) Wells (1866-1946) held a more optimistic view of history. Where Marx's analysis centered on revolution, Wells's centered on evolution. Instead of violent upheaval as an agent of social change, Wells envisioned the gradual development of society into better forms.

Much of Wells's mental energy was directed toward the future, and some of his futuristic novels, such as *The Time Machine* and *War of the Worlds*, have become classics. In his *magnum opus*, *The Outline of History* (1922), Wells sees the fledgling League of Nations as a hopeful first step toward developing a world government: "Our true State, this state that is already beginning, this state to which every man owes his utmost political effort, must be now this nascent Federal World State to which human necessities point" (1290). Even in the aftermath of the Great War—an event so devastating to others—he is persistently optimistic: "We believe in the power of reason and in the increasing good-will in men" (1290). At the same time Wells's post-Enlightenment optimism is necessarily tempered by the realities of the recent war; he sees the darker nature in man and foresees a long struggle to develop the better world (1290).

How will that brave new world come into being? Unlike either Marx or Spengler, Wells introduces the possibilities of religion as a force for the unity of mankind, as opposed to the kind of competitive denominationalism that fueled the national rivalries that had so recently erupted into war: "Our true God now is the God of all men. Nationalism as a God must follow the tribal gods to limbo. Our true nationality is mankind" (1290). Religion for Wells plays a key part in the development of a new world order. "The coming world state . . . will be based upon a common world religion, very much simplified and universalized and better understood. This will not be Christianity or Islam or Buddhism nor any such specialized form of religion, but religion itself pure and undefiled" (1297).

Wells sees the classroom as an agent of social change. "This world state will be sustained by a universal education. . . . The whole race, and not simply classes and peoples, will be *educated*" (1297). That is, the tenets of a world religion and a world state will be catechized into the populace through universal, ongoing education. A world religion will serve the world state, and the world state will benevolently serve the people. The result will be the progress of the human race. As to that progress, Wells gushes about the possibilities: "Only the spirit-lessness of our present depression blinds us to the clear intimations of our reason that in the course of a few generations every little country town could become an Athens, every human being could be gentle in breeding and healthy in body and mind, the whole solid earth man's mine and its uttermost regions his playground" (1301).

The implication here is that traditional, orthodox Christianity, with its specific affirmations and anathemas, had better not stand in the way of progress. Or else. In contrast to Wells's thought, the Christian faith is at the same time realistic and optimistic on the basis of scriptural truth. The Church is realistic about the true nature of man, reasoning from the doctrine of Original Sin. With St. Paul, we recognize that in us—that is, in our sinful flesh—there is nothing good. At the same time, we have this hope of glory in us, with the Holy Spirit given to us as a constant, indwelling down payment of the eternal trea-sures that await us in a heaven of unending joy and peace. While liv-ing in this paradox, we work to improve this world as much as we can while recognizing that we have here no abiding habitation.

Toynbee

The historian Arnold Joseph Toynbee (1889-1975), like Spengler, noted the increased interest in the future during uncertain times: "As a rule, people feel acute concern about the future, beyond the horizon of the present, only when the times are out of joint. In our generation, we are living in one of these times of unusually intense stress and anxiety. What awaits us?" (3). Like Wells, Toynbee answers that question by envisioning a world government: "We can, in fact, foresee a world . . . in which a human being's . . . paramount political allegiance will be given to mankind as a whole and to the literally world-wide world-state" (87).

President Ronald Reagan was heard to quip, "*Status quo* is Latin for 'the mess we're in.'" If the times are out of joint as Toynbee says (alluding to Hamlet), how did we get into this mess? He notes that the Catholic-Protestant religious wars of the sixteenth and seventeenth centuries led to the decline of Christianity in the West and to the rise of Rationalism in the eighteenth century (170). The resulting spiritual vacuum brought about the three competing secular substitutes for Christianity: Nationalism, Individualism, and Communism. These, he argues, are inadequate substitutes for religion (176). Nationalism, such as witnessed in Nazi Germany, is particularly dangerous. "The antidote to Nationalism is world-mindedness; and the two historical institutions in which this world-mindedness has found expression are the would-be world-states and world-religions" (112).

As for a world state, Toynbee, after analyzing various empires of the past and present, interestingly concludes that China has the most potential for creating a workable, unified world government, though a government not of force. The idea is, get the U.N. out of the U.S. and move it to Beijing.

But Toynbee diverges from Wells in that he does not see the same need for a unified world religion that he does for a world government: "A plurality and variety of religions will be desirable in a politically unified state" (195). He names Christianity, Buddhism, and Islam as the three great missionary higher religions of the world, noting that they succeeded in unifying large portions of the human race but failed because of schism and oppression. Toynbee calls Zoroastrianism, Judaism, and Hinduism higher religions (as opposed to primitive tribal cults), but relegates them to lesser status because they remained yoked to the communities in which they originated, never breaking out of their ethnic enclaves and becoming a dominant influence in other cultures (161).

Writing in the Sixties, Toynbee approved of the newly emerging and more positive signs for a future of religious diversity and toleration, with each faith realizing that the other is but one of many possible approaches to truth. The Protestant ecumenical movement was cresting just at this time. Pope John XXIII had initiated Vatican II not long before, ratifying a liberal movement in the Roman Catholic Church toward cooperation as opposed to its more traditional competition with other religions. Then Pope Paul VI conducted visits to Muslim and Hindu lands, receiving enthusiastic receptions by adherents of faiths very different from his own (177-178).

Like Marx and Wells, Toynbee builds on Darwin in foreseeing a future for the human race of two billion years. He seems to reflect an affinity for Eastern thought in seeing this long future history as cyclic, something eminently possible given a practically infinite future within which civilizations could develop. He notes that the old Ottoman Empire was successful because it allowed for religious toleration and diversity within the external structure of a unified multicultural state. It was subdivided into religious districts, or "millets," which enfranchised Jewish and Christian regions within the Islamic body politic (188). As the current cycle of Western civilization rolls forward, Toynbee argues, the Ottoman Empire will provide a paradigm for "the new oecumenical society into which all sections of mankind are moving in our time" (189).

The flaw in Toynbee is the same as in the Enlightenment: vanity. Seeing the future in terms of its own urbanity. "Since [the eighteenth century] the Modern Western outlook has become the outlook of a world-wide Westernizing intelligentsia; and what the intelligentsia thinks today, the masses will think tomorrow. The Western mind's insistence on thinking for itself and putting traditional doctrines to the test thus seems to be the 'wave of the future' for the world" (187). In other words, in the future everybody will be just like Arnold J. Toynbee.

There is a grain of truth in each of these philosophers of history. Factory owners do often exploit labor unfairly. Civilizations do come to an end. There really have been some improvements that have come to benefit the human race. Patterns in history, cycles in culture, do exist.

Christian thinkers have also worked in this area. Francis A. Schaeffer attempted an analysis of Western civilization since the Reformation in the book and film series *How Should We Then Live?* Oxford-educated Os Guinness, a former student of Schaeffer's at the L'Abri Fellowship in Switzerland, critiques the ills of our sick society in *The Dust of Death*. Herbert Schlossberg, in *Idols for Destruction*, argues for a thoroughgoing Christian transformation of society. *Postmodern Times* by Gene Edward Veith outlines pervasive cultural maladies such as the loss of absolute values and the erosion of meaning.

Sorokin

While all of the above are valuable studies, none quite encompasses the scope of the work of Pitirim A. Sorokin (1889-1968). This Russian émigré was founder and chairman of the Department of Sociology at Harvard, 1930-1944. The most eminent sociologist of his generation, Sorokin came from the older, more prophetic school of sociology, proceeding not only by research but intuition, prediction, and rebuke. He was ousted in a no-holds-barred academic fight by Talcott Parsons, a rising academic star who expounded the newer, more statistical/descriptive approach to sociology. In time the Parsons school succeeded in almost completely eliminating Sorokin's influence. That is why you will probably find Parsons listed in your encyclopedia but not Sorokin. More recently, however, Sorokin is being rediscovered as time has validated many of his predictions (Brown, Johnston).

While Sorokin is not an apologist for the Christian faith *per se*, the outlines of his thought—unlike those of Marx, Spengler, Wells, or

Toynbee (who was a friend and admirer of Sorokin's)—generally fall within a Christian framework. He does not envision a unified world religion, much less a world state. Having grown up in Russia where he was thrown in jail once by Czar Nicholas and once by Lenin, he was deeply suspicious of totalitarianism in any form. Moreover, he excludes any syncretistic world religion like that envisioned by Wells or even an equalization of competing world religions like that described by Toynbee. In fact, the final sentence of his *The Crisis of Our Age* (1941) is, "*Benedicite qui venit in nomine Domini*" ("Blessed is He who comes in the name of the Lord"), a clear reference to the Second Coming of Christ.

Like most European intellectuals, Sorokin had believed in the idea of enlightened human progress; and like most European intellectuals, his faith in such cultural evolution was shattered by World War I. His personal crisis led him as a professional sociologist to undertake a scientific inquiry into systems of culture. Spengler's *Decline of the West* was much in vogue in the Twenties, but Sorokin had the idea that Western civilization, though deeply troubled, was perhaps not coming to a complete and final end. His hypothesis was rather that twentieth-century Western society was going through a turbulent but limited period of transition between two major cultural systems, which he calls the Sensate and the Ideational. He argued that the crisis would deepen and continue through the twentieth century but eventually resolve itself into a new mode of civilization very different from that which had characterized the Modern Era.

To test this hypothesis, Sorokin recruited teams of researchers, each team having a different area of academic expertise. To each he assigned the task of researching a different area of human activity, to see if there were any variations or patterns over the past thirty centuries of Western civilization. To none did he communicate his general theory; each team was working independently. These groups investigated trends in major cultural indicators such as the fine arts, science, philosophy, religion, ethics, law, family, government, criminality, and war. As the results began to come in, Sorokin found his hypothesis confirmed by the evidence. He began to publish his findings in the 1920s, culminating in his *magnum opus, Social and Cultural Dynamics* (1937).

Sorokin's theory is that Western civilization has experienced major cultural movement over a period of many centuries, oscillating slowly between two modes, which he called the Sensate and the Ideational. In the Sensate cultural mode, true reality is sensory. Material values predominate. An example of this would be the Roman Empire. Its focus was on practical matters such as efficient systems of government, the military, transportation, communication, sanitation, and so forth. At the opposite pole is the Ideational cultural mode. In this system, true reality is supersensory. Spiritual values predominate. An example of this would be the Christian Middle Ages. The central organizing authority was not the state but the Church. The most important buildings were constructed for religious purposes. Many men and women abandoned the pursuit of material gain in order to devote their lives to prayer in monasteries. A proliferation of religious festivals kept the people focused on the world to come, to the detriment of the economy.

Both systems at their peak tend to be stable and relatively long lasting. The Roman Empire really did hang together rather well for about 700 years, and the *Pax Romana* remains in our vocabulary as a proverbial period of world peace. Likewise the stasis of the Medieval World produced a long period of Christian civilization in which the arts of architecture, theology, education, and liturgy reached a high degree of development.

During each period of dominance of one of these cultural modes, there are representatives of what Sorokin calls "the unintegrated opposite principle." That is, in each historical period there is both a dominant and recessive mode. The Sensate continues in an Ideational phase but as a weaker influence. During a Sensate phase, the Ideational is still present but not as strong. There were saints in Rome, skeptics in the Middle Ages. It's never all one or the other—entirely Sensate or entirely Ideational. Nor does either cultural mode stay in ascendancy for an indefinite period of time. Each carries within itself the seeds of its own decay, leading to periods of transition. Sensate Rome got bigger and louder and more and more worldly, and as its decadent phase accelerated, the representatives of the unintegrated opposite principle—in this case the religiously-minded Christians—gathered momentum and moved into ascendancy.

Sorokin calls these periods of change Idealistic. For our purposes here I will use the simpler and less confusing term, Transitional. In these periods cultural values are partly sensory, partly supersensory. These are times in which indicators of cultural dislocation and social upheaval are intensified: more wars, revolutions, suicides, divorces, delinquency, and crime. They are also times of great artistic achievement. An example of such a Transitional period would be what has come to be called the Dark Ages (the term was actually coined by Petrarch in the fourteenth century), when Sensate Rome was declining and the Ideational Christian Church was on the rise. It was during this time that rhyming was introduced into Western poetry by St. Ambrose as a way to help Christians memorize religious verse. Another would be that period variously referred to as the Reformation and the Renaissance, in which the Ideational Medieval World was giving way to the Sensate Modern Era. The achievement of the poet Shakespeare needs no comment. It is also interesting to note that the sharpened eschatological expectations of St. Augustine (c. 400) and Martin Luther (c. 1500) occurred just during these periods of transition.

Our own twentieth century, Sorokin argued, is also one of these periods of transition between two major cultural systems as the Sensate Modern Era is breaking up and our civilization is moving into a more Ideational cultural mode. A spiritual society is emerging. In a way these Transitional periods between large cultural systems are like the shorter transitional seasons of Spring and Fall—partly warm and partly cool—that move us from the longer, more unified seasons of Winter and Summer. To use another image, time is like a river that

Figure 1:
Chart of Cultural Dynamics in Western Civilization

Year:	800	600	400	BC + AD	400	1000	1500	1600	1700	1800	1900	2000
Culture:	Greek	transition	Roman		trans.	Medieval	trans.			Modern	trans.	Therian
				CHRIST								
Poet:	Homer	Aeschylus	Virgil		Beowulf	Dante		Shakespeare	Pope	Wordsworth	Eliot	

Mode: Ideational

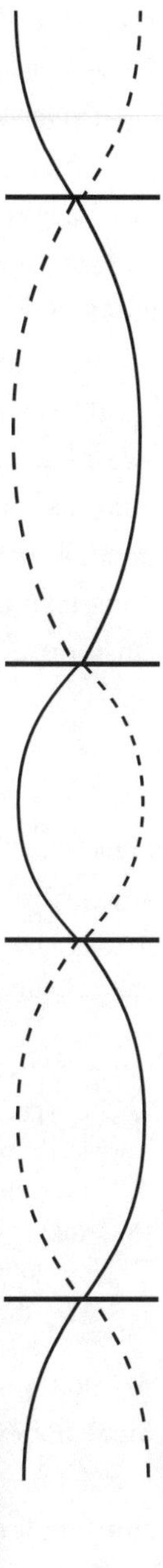

Mode: Sensate

flows along at a constant rate. But in the river there are warm and cold currents. Now one is near the surface, now another, as anyone who has swum in a river knows very well. Where the currents cross, there is turbulence.

We can envision cultural change in this way (see Figure 1). Here we see an overview of Western civilization from the time of the Greeks to the present. The wavy lines represent the two cultural modes, Ideational and Sensate. Where they cross, there is a period of Transition. I am also positing a sequence of symbolic events to demarcate cultural shifts. The criteria for each is that it be universally known and also stand as a metaphor for the period in which it occurs. The fall of Rome in 476, for example, stands as a symbol for the end of a great and long-standing Sensate era and the beginning of a turbulent time of Transition.

Figure 2:
Chart of Symbolic Events

Date	Event	Significance	Text page #
323 B.C.	Conquest of Alexander	End of Transition, beginning of Sensate period	p. 55
476 A.D.	Fall of Rome	End of Sensate period, beginning of Transition	p. 55
800	Coronation of Charlemagne	End of Transition, beginning of Ideational period	p. 101
1492	Voyage of Columbus	End of Ideational period, beginning of Transition	p. 117
1641	Descartes: *Cogito ergo sum*	End of Transition, beginning of Sensate period	p. 126
1912	Sinking of the *Titanic*	End of Sensate period, beginning of Transition	p. 131
1969	Woodstock Music Festival	End of Transition, beginning of Ideational Period	p. 155

In attempting to understand the times in regard to major cultural trends, one must give attention to the importance of the fine arts.

Indeed, Sorokin's teams studied over 100,000 works of art and literature from the Middle Ages to 1930. To answer the question that everybody wants to know, art mirrors society. It does not shape it. Shelley called poets the "unacknowledged legislators of the world" (Abrams, I, 765). The evidence does not seem to bear this out, even though the arts do constitute the best indicator we have of cultural trends. What is going on in society is always reflected in the arts. Just when everything else seems to be going wrong in America, says poet Charles Simic, "poetry is doing just fine. . . . Poetry is always the cat concert under the window of the room in which the official version of reality is being written. . . . But what if the poets are not crazy? What if they convey the feel of a historical period better than anybody else?" (Bloom, 353).

With this in mind, we can see the differences between the major cultural modes in terms of the arts. Ideational art tends to be symbolic, static, and focused on spiritual or supersensory things. Sensate art, by contrast, tends to be concrete, dynamic, and stimulating to the senses. Compare a medieval chant with a Beethoven symphony and you begin to get the picture. Or a Byzantine icon with a painting by Rubens. The chant and the icon are static and anonymous, carefully designed to uplift the spirit and impart religious meaning through symbol. By contrast, we know the names of Beethoven and Rubens; their work, while crafted with equal care, is dynamic and powerful, leading the listener or viewer to an experience of emotional intensity.

It is important to note that we experience a fairly uniform culture on both sides of the Atlantic. Sorokin never speculates about the deeper underlying causes, but demonstrates that both Europe and America are on about the same cultural timetable. Rationalism appears in Europe, England, and America in the eighteenth century, Romanticism in the nineteenth, Modernism in the twentieth.

I do not agree with everything Sorokin says. A flaw in Sorokin's outlook is an implied postmillennial eschatology. He seems to envision a coming Ideational phase of our culture as setting up a spiritual realm something like the kingdom of God, a renewal of Christian culture that will culminate in the Return of Christ (Johnston, 147). In addition, there is in Sorokin a strain of mysticism that is not tethered to reality—as if he himself were a harbinger of the new Ideational man.

Still, Sorokin goes farther and deeper than anyone else in his analysis of Western culture. He is a helpful guide in analyzing large systems of cultural change over long periods of time, in helping us understand the times—where we have come from and where we are today and where we may be going. The things he predicted in the Twenties—that the era of dictators and war and social upheaval would continue, that the War to End All Wars was only a beginning of troubles in a declining Sensate culture—have certainly come to pass. Furthermore, he may give us a clue as to what is coming next. If he is right, we are now seeing the beginnings of a new Ideational phase, a time of renewed interest in spiritual things. Unlike the Middle Ages, however, this new dominant spirituality, which I call the "Therian Age" (see Chapter Eight), will not be particularly friendly toward the Christian faith. And for Christians who insist on the ancient truths, it will not be a pleasant time. We will remain where we have been all along—and where we truly ought to be in Christ—under the cross.

3

Western Civ. 101

Building upon the theoretical framework of Sorokin and others, we begin to derive a broad overview of Western civilization. If we get into a balloon, so to speak, and go up high enough, we can start to get the cultural lay of the land—how the rivers connect with the fields, what the shape of the forest is, and where the mountains are—much in the way that military strategists use aircraft for reconnaissance.

Sorokin argues that the civilization of the Greeks was Ideational, a period of time in which dominant cultural values were supersensory. As this culture fell into decline, it went through a Transitional period in which sensory values mixed with the supersensory. Greek civilization was supplanted by the more Sensate Roman Empire. The dominant cultural values of Rome were materialistic or sensory. As Sensate Rome declined, there ensued a Transitional period in which the dominant modes of cultural expression were partly Sensate and partly Ideational—that is, partly materialistic and partly spiritual—but moving steadily toward the alternate mode. These so-called Dark Ages saw the rise and establishment of the Christian faith in the West. The Middle Ages were Ideational, a time in which cultural values were predominantly spiritual. The rise of commerce and material values in the declining Middle Ages led to a Transitional period we call the Renaissance.

The Modern Period swung to the Sensate mode again—an era ruled by the physical sciences, with empirical evidence as the criterion for all truth, an era of tangible, practical achievement in the material world. It will be seen that the Sensate, Modern Era has been in decline for some time. We now seem to be in a turbulent Transitional period, heading rapidly into a new Ideational mode. This view becomes clear if we go up in the balloon and take a broad overview of cultural history in terms of Sensate/Ideational modality (see Figure 1 on page 47). As we look at each epoch, it will be seen that the arts, in particular the poetry of a given period, are accurate indicators of its dominant cultural mode. We will also see the influence of the Gospel of Jesus Christ throughout.

Greece: Ideational

The culture of the Greeks, at its height from about the eighth to the sixth centuries B.C., may be interpreted as having been predominantly Ideational. The sculpture of Praxiteles is stylized, not at all realistic. Pythagoras, after whom the mathematical theorem is named, was more religious philosopher than mathematician. He traveled East to Babylon and absorbed much of their mystical wisdom, including theories of the transmigration of the soul that he imparted to the members of his secret society. Plato wrestled with concepts of pure abstraction.

In the epic poetry of Homer, men and gods freely interact. *The Iliad*, the epic poem about the fall of Troy, begins with an invocation: "Sing, O Goddess" (3). This might be put down as the poetic convention of beseeching the inspiration of a muse, but as the narrative proceeds it becomes clear that the unseen realm hovers near the visible actions of mankind. When an argument arises between Achilles and Agamemnon the poet asks, "Which of the gods was it that set them on to quarrel?" (3). The problem had begun when Agamemnon dishonored the priest Chryses by refusing the ransom offered to free the priest's daughter. This angered Apollo, the god whom the priest served. Chryses prayed for vengeance: "Thus did he pray, and Apollo heard his prayer. He came down, furious from the summits of Olympus" (3). Achilles, the friend of Chryses, is enraged at Agamemnon's greed and pride. But just as he is ready to draw his sword, "Minerva came down from heaven . . . visible to him alone" (5). She counseled him to control his anger. "Goddess," answered Achilles, "however angry a man may be, he must do as you . . . command him. This will be best, for the gods ever hear the prayers of him who has obeyed them" (5).

The story continues in this manner to its end, illustrating the universal precept that "so were the counsels of Jove fulfilled" (3). For the sake of comparison and to illustrate the tonal difference between Ideational and Sensate art, can you imagine such elements as these in a short story in a modern literary magazine like *The New Yorker*? A submission written in this vein would never make it past the slush pile. Homer's poetry gives a window into a completely different world, one of close relations between men and their gods. Or should we say the gods and their men. There is a kind of pagan determinism here: We are what we do, often the gods make us do what we do, and we must endure the consequences of our actions, be they good or evil. There is a one-for-one correspondence between human action and its reward, with fate, or the will of the gods, as the ultimate determiner. Right or wrong, that is the worldview reflected in the poetry. The gods on Mount Olympus rule the world below, and men interact with them closely. But if we could find something like *The New Yorker* that had been published, say, by Dante and his circle of *literati* in medieval Italy, we might find just this sort of intimacy between heaven and earth.

One might ask what impact, if any, the Greek world had on the progress of the Gospel when the Gospel was yet unknown in the West. I would observe briefly that the spread of the Greek language throughout the Mediterranean world during the conquests of Alexander the Great (356-323 B.C.) certainly prepared the way for universal transmission of the Good News of Jesus Christ. But on the negative side, the notion of a personal relationship with a supernatural being like Achilles had had eventually filtered through Roman civilization and found its way into the saint worship of the Roman church. Instead of one mediator between God and man, the Roman Catholic Church set forth many: You prayed to St. Christopher before going on a trip; St. Mary replaced Hera, wife of Zeus, as chief female deity, the one you had to go through to present your requests to God. As we look at this era we should keep one important point in view, especially as we consider what might be coming after Postmodernism: An Ideational culture can be spiritual without being Christian. In fact, it can be positively antagonistic toward Christianity.

Transition: Ideational to Sensate

New modes of cultural expression come into Greece with a Transitional period from around the sixth to the fifth centuries B.C., pointing ahead to a more Sensate Roman civilization. The philosopher Aristotle, trained as a botanist, was less interested in pure abstractions than his predecessor Plato. In the *Poetics*, Aristotle defines the concrete elements that make good drama, particularly the character-centered concept of the tragic flaw.

It is during this time that Aeschylus introduces a new realism into Greek dramatic poetry, establishing the five-act, character-centered dramaturgy that was rediscovered during the Renaissance—perhaps not surprising since the Renaissance was also a Transitional period moving from an Ideational to a Sensate cultural mode—and prevails to this day, even in Hollywood movies. In *Agamemnon*, a tragedy that deals with some of the same characters as the *Iliad*, the gods are conspicuously absent from the *dramatis personae*. In the Prologue the Chorus describes the background of the play. It is the immediate aftermath of the fall of Troy. But there is scant reference to the gods. It is the motives and actions of men that are at play here. Is there a note of skepticism in the line, "Zeus—whosoe'er He be" (53)? Aeschylus writes with a completely different point of view than Homer. He is more secular. Gone are the constant references to the gods and their interactions with men on an ongoing basis. There is a disturbingly decadent aspect about Troy. "Paris . . . for fair welcome left foul shame, / And stole away the wedded wife" (56). Paris ran off with Helen, a married woman, and in so doing touched off the armed conflict. Paris did it on his own. He is not a pawn of the gods.

Still, in Aeschylus there are references to divine influence. The Herald speaks of "Hermes, my Defence" and extols "the grace of Zeus that wrought these things" (57-58). In sum, the Greek playwrights show us a poetry rich in contemplation of human motive and action, but one through which there runs a strong undercurrent of the old religion. It is a pagan religion, to be sure, but one in which the power of the ancient gods is more at a balance with the new power of human will.

In indication to cultural indicators, Greek civilization showed a more Sensate direction with the military exploits of Alexander the Great. The completion of his conquests that ended with his death in 323 B.C. must stand as a symbolic event for the end of a Transition and the beginning of a new Sensate era (see Figure 2, p. 48).

Rome: Sensate

The Roman Empire, dominant in the West from about the fourth century B.C. to the fourth century A.D., is unquestionably Sensate in its preoccupations. As previously noted, the Roman mind worked toward improvements of the existing order. One is continually amazed at the practical amenities of daily living produced by the Romans, many of which were lost after the Empire's collapse—plumbing, hot baths, good roads and bridges.

This Sensate orientation is reflected likewise in the arts. Roman sculpture, often titanic in size, is more realistic than symbolic. Julius

Caesar is depicted as he is: bald. The title of Ovid's book, *The Art of Love*, speaks for itself. No metaphysical speculation here.

Virgil, the greatest Latin poet, reflects a preoccupation with practical matters in his epic poem, *The Aeneid*. Virgil calls him "pious" Aeneas. This patriarch of the Romans has escaped from burning Troy, bearing his aged father Anchises on his back. With a cohort of loyal men, he sets sail for parts unknown. On the journey we find much attention to details of the natural world, something not as prevalent in previous writers: "At length to Libya's coast they come. There is a spot / Deep in a cove's recess: an isle there makes / A harbour with the barrier of its sides, / 'Gainst which no deep-sea billow is but dashed, / And sundered far into sequestered creeks" (107).

Amidst all the intrigues, adventures, and battles, Book VI stands as the philosophical center of *The Aeneid*. Here we find the poet concerned with the administration of a just society. Traditionally, poets are the natural guardians of moral values in a society. Their function is not unlike that of the biblical prophets—many of whom were surpassingly good poets. Poets and prophets stood in the civilization with the call to use words creatively to instruct the people and, if necessary, rebuke the king. Caesar Augustus—the same one named in the second chapter of Luke—was Virgil's patron; Virgil was Augustus' teacher, entrusted with the young man's moral formation. So the poet works the instruction into the story.

Aeneas visits the Sibyl to get a vision of the future, then goes to the underworld to see the shade of his departed father. There he encounters shades in torment for sins committed while alive on earth, providing powerful moral lessons of vices to avoid. It is easy to see why Dante chose Virgil as his guide through the lower regions. In Hades, Aeneas sees Deiphobus, "sore mangled all his frame, / Face and both hands rent cruelly, his ears / From the maimed temples shorn" (224). Aghast, Aeneas asks what happened. Deiphobus tells him that it was a "Laconian woman plunged me in this woe" because of "treacherous joys" indulged in far into the night (224). Moral: A virtuous leader, like Augustus, must avoid entanglements with the opposite sex. Poor Phlegyas, "wretchedest of men," cries out with a loud voice in a kind of summary statement, "Be taught, learn justice, and spurn not the gods" (227).

In Virgil and other classical authors there is much encoded virtue to learn and emulate. Luther expressed the opinion that it was because of their superior virtue that God gave an empire to the Romans, an empire whose political stability and infrastructure facilitated the spread of Christianity. One can readily see why generations of English schoolboys were forced to learn Greek and Latin and grind their way through the "Greats." They, like Augustus, were being prepared to rule an empire. But we are dealing here with the wisdom of the pagan mind. It is practical wisdom, and it comes from sound minds, but there is not a whisper of the mystery that cannot be grasped by human reason unaided by divine revelation. Even as Augustus ruled well, guided by Virgil, this wisdom from above was being articulated in an obscure corner of the Empire. It was a wisdom that would soon break out of Judea and turn the whole Roman world upside down, even as the seeds of decay inherent in the Sensate culture began to sprout and bear bitter fruit.

Transition: Sensate to Ideational

The popular imagination often associates the Roman Empire with its late decadent phase. Images of drunken sex orgies, spectacular entertainments in the Colosseum, gladiator contests, and of course Christians being fed to the lions are firmly planted in the modern mind. These things did happen. A Sensate culture tends not to moderate itself with spiritual principles; it rather gradually progresses to its logical extremity, becoming more and more Sensate. In a way, the career of Marc Antony is symbolic of the progress and subsequent decline of the Empire itself. A soldier of outstanding valor and military skill and a member of the Second Triumvirate (44-30 B.C.),

Antony gave himself over in his middle age to sensual indulgence in the arms of a still-charming Cleopatra. The resulting chaos drew other members of the Triumvirate into battle with Antony. Defeated, he fell on his sword.

The infamous Nero (d. A.D. 68) actually began his reign quite auspiciously and ruled well for some time. Only later did he plunge into a life of shocking immorality. Threatened by the rising tide of Christianity, Nero initiated the first of the ten persecutions and also ordered the executions of Saints Peter and Paul. He was succeeded by many otherwise capable administrators, but the irreversible decline actually began with the reign of the evil Commodus (d. 192), the emperor featured in the recent film, *Gladiator*. In reality, he was murdered by the Praetorian Guard, who then auctioned off the office of emperor to the highest bidder. The die was cast. One bad emperor followed another, significantly weakening the strength of the civilization.

It is important to note that official persecutions against the Church—like those in China today—were for the most part intermittent and regional. The government could not have sustained a universal and ongoing effort to exterminate the Church (it had other matters to attend to, such as a rising military threat from German tribes to the north), nor could the Church have withstood it. Still, during the early years of the Church, the Gospel was opposed by external forces. The last and worst persecution was initiated by Diocletian. It was universal and lasted ten years (A.D. 303-313). Shortly afterwards, in 314, Constantine became the first Christian emperor; and while he did not make Christianity the religion of the Empire as is often thought, he did grant it official toleration and ended for the time all persecution and external opposition to the Gospel of Jesus Christ.

Constantine moved the imperial capitol from Rome to Constantinople (formerly Byzantium, today Istanbul). Still, the Eternal City remained symbolically important to what was left of the Empire. Christian emperors struggled to hold the civilization together, but there was too much territory to govern and too few troops and capable administrators. From then on Roman institutions crumbled rapidly until the unimaginable happened—Rome was sacked by the Goths in 410. From then on disaster followed disaster until 476, the generally accepted date for the Fall of Rome. After 476 there were no more Roman emperors. This devastating event must stand as symbolic for the end of the Roman Sensate era and the beginning of a new Transitional period (see Figure 2, p. 48).

As the Roman Empire crumbled, a more spiritually-minded Christian civilization began to emerge in the fifth to seventh centuries A.D. That this Transitional period has come to be commonly described as "dark" is surely due to the Sensate perspective of the Modern Era. The glory that was Rome was no more, a loss felt deeply by secular man. The Empire continued in a fashion in the East. But with Eastern sensibilities and the influence of the Church, it was a far cry from what it had been under the caesars.

So in the West it is called the Dark Ages. But it was during this time that the light of the Gospel of Jesus Christ continued to spread rapidly among the pagan tribes of Europe. Missionary monks preached everywhere. St. Columba brought the Gospel to the savages of Britain. St. Patrick converted the pagan tribes of Ireland. St. Boniface had the audacity to chop down a sacred oak. Unharmed by the tree's god, he brought Christ to the uncivilized Germans.

In poetry, *Beowulf* was written down—an epic that appears pagan at first glance, until the Christian reader begins to see the spiritual foundation of the poem. The hero Beowulf, like Jesus, defeats a monster, gives gifts unto his men, and dies a redemptive death. The monster Grendel is described as a "kin of Cain" (Abrams, I, 28). Hence, for Beowulf to fight this monster is at once to reenact the ancient struggle between good and evil. In the fight, Beowulf, like young David against Goliath, lays aside his arms in order to better trust God for the outcome: "We shall forgo the sword in the night . . . and then may wise God, Holy Lord, assign glory on whichever hand seems good to him" (36). By the grace of God, Beowulf defeats the monster, Grendel.

Late in Beowulf's life, he must face another manifestation of evil, "the smooth hateful dragon who flies at night wrapped in flame" (56). In the battle, Beowulf is wounded but slays the dragon, just as Christ in his death defeats the devil. The dragon has guarded a hoard of treasure, which the king now plunders. With his last breath the old king gives glory to God: "I speak with my words thanks to the Lord of All for these treasures, to the King of Glory, Eternal Prince, for what I gaze on here, that I might get such for my people before my death-day. Now that I have bought the hoard of treasures with my old life, you attend to the people's needs hereafter" (63). Like Christ, in his sacrificial death for the benefit of his people, he leaves them endowed with riches. Beowulf is buried with great honor by his people and is lamented: "He was of world-kings the mildest of men and the gentlest, kindest to his people, and most eager for fame" (68). To be "eager for fame" is not to say that he was filled with pride. Rather, he was willing to risk his life in battle for the good of his people. At the same time, he is admired for his Christlike virtues. Beowulf is meek and mild like a good shepherd-king toward his subjects, but monsters and dragons find his visage quite intimidating.

In this epic poem, Christian and pagan values swirl and mix in the turbulent crosscurrent of a Transitional period in Western civilization. Courage in combat, willingness to endure hardship . . . these virtues of a Viking culture linger in Old English poetry. Yet there is here, as in the Ring trilogy of J. R. R. Tolkien—an Oxford English professor and a world expert on *Beowulf*—a strong undercurrent of the Christian faith running swift and strong right under the surface.

What was emerging in the West was a predominantly Ideational or Christian phase of culture. The spiritual elements would be the harbinger of the future. With the cessation of governmental persecution and the advance of spiritual cultural values, opposition to the Gospel would assume new forms. The attacks would now be spiritual in nature. Therefore we must take note of the heretical ideas that arose to challenge the progress of the pure Gospel of Jesus Christ. In a rising Ideational phase of civilization, the greatest threats to the Gospel will be likewise Ideational. St. Paul seems to recognize this threat when he says, "Our struggle is not against flesh and blood, but against the rulers, against the authorities, against the powers of this dark world and against the spiritual forces of evil in the heavenly realms" (Ephesians 6:12). Those spiritual forces of evil always find a way to get inside the Church and disrupt the progress of the Gospel from within.

4

The Church

Keeping Sorokin's model of cultural change in mind, it is interesting to note that the Christian faith arose during a Transitional period of Western civilization—that is, one in which both material and spiritual values were in roughly equal balance. Indeed, one can make the case that Christianity is a balance of both Ideational and Sensate elements. In Jesus Christ, God became flesh. In the resurrection, the believer's body will be redeemed along with the soul. The worship of the Church revolves not only around the preaching of the Word of God, but rituals that engage the body with material elements: water, bread and wine. We will find in this chapter that the heresies that have fought against the Word of God have often tried to disrupt this mysterious and paradoxical balance of spiritual and material things in the Christian faith. In the next chapter we will look at Islam, Christianity's greatest challenge, a religion that is almost entirely superspiritual. Looking further ahead, we will see that the newly emerging Ideational phase of Western culture will probably be very spiritual but not at all compatible with or friendly toward Christianity.

"Fighting and fears without, within," the Church sings in the old hymn. And in another she frankly admits that there are "false sons

within her pale." If attacks on the truth from outside the church are
not enough, there are constant challenges from the inside. Within each
individual believer there is a little doubter, a little self-righteous
Pharisee, a little skeptical Pilate asking sarcastically, "What is truth?"
From time to time men arise to organize opposition to the truth of
God's Word and lead many astray. In an unusual verse—interestingly,
in the context of his famous passage on the Lord's Supper—St. Paul
says, "No doubt there have to be differences [Greek: *haireses*, literally,
"heresies"] among you to show which of you have God's approval"
(1 Corinthians 11:19). Perhaps God in His infinite wisdom allows
heretics to arise from certain quarters within the Church so that the
truth may be defined for the greater good of the whole. This has certainly been the case down through the centuries, as councils and individuals have stood up at critical moments for the clear teaching of the
Word of God.

Some look back to the time of the first-century apostles as a kind
of "golden age" of the Church, a period of ongoing revival when
doctrine was pure, preaching fervent, and miracles commonplace.
Then everything went wrong for the better part of 2,000 years until
the revivals of the twentieth century restored true Christianity to the
earth. This assumption is false. A glance at the Bible shows that the
truth was contested from the beginning, and a look at church history shows that the truth—though continually opposed—was preserved through all centuries. In all instances, the heretical attack and
the Church's response have centered in the one doctrine upon which
the Church stands or falls: justification by faith alone, that simple
declaration that all have sinned but are saved not by their own
works but by God's work, by faith in the death and resurrection of
Jesus Christ. That is the Gospel, at one and the same time the clear-
est teaching in the Bible and the most misunderstood, the common-
est thing in the Church and also the most rare, the doctrine most
loved by those who worship Christ and most hated by those who
would lift up man.

The Jews

First to oppose the Gospel were naturally the Jews, those most threatened by its implications. In first-century Jerusalem the Pharisees and Sadducees were firmly in control of the religious allegiance of the people. The Pharisees held power through their teaching of works-righteousness, the Sadducees through management of the temple and its lucrative system of sacrifices. Jesus of Nazareth was a threat to them. He had called them what they were: whitewashed tombs, outwardly beautiful but inside full of dead men's bones. They knew He was the Messiah. No question about that—His miracles attested to His divinity, not to mention the authority of His teaching. In the hardness of their hearts—their persistence in unbelief against all evidence was almost miraculous—they perversely went against their consciences and better knowledge and had Him destroyed. They meant it for evil, but God meant it for good, for in the death of Christ, death was destroyed, the sin of the world was paid for, and mankind was redeemed. In the glory of His resurrection, God declared Christ innocent and just, validated all of His teaching, and proved to the world that this was truly the Son of God.

Someone once compared the death and resurrection of Jesus Christ to the Normandy Invasion of World War II. At that moment the war was won, though the Germans fought back savagely and much blood remained to be shed on the Allies' march to Berlin. But for the Nazis from then on it was a lost cause. Their doom was sealed. In the same way Jesus spoke truly on the eve of His arrest when He said, "The prince of this world now stands condemned" (John 16:11). Christ's death and resurrection broke the power of the devil, put him in chains, and limited his power to deceive the nations. Henceforth the key to history would be not the progress of satanic deception but the advance of the Holy Gospel. When Christ sent the Holy Spirit at Pentecost it was an overpowering force, like the fresh and well-armed troops pouring into France through Omaha Beach.

Satan was from the beginning a murderer and a liar. Perhaps he even deceives himself into believing that he can still win. His attack is always upon the Gospel in one way or another, for that is the doctrine upon which not only the kingdom of God but also the kingdom of darkness stands or falls. This is not an oversimplification. Scripture says that "we are not unaware of [Satan's] schemes" (2 Corinthians 2:11). After all these centuries of battle we, like old generals, know our adversary well. He behaves in certain predictable ways. He is vulnerable to the preaching of the cross. That is where he will marshal his forces. Certainly he has had notable victories along the way and has never been at a loss for human instruments through which to weave his web of deceit.

It didn't take long for him to organize opposition to the fledgling Church. Shortly after Pentecost, Peter and John—still observing temple rites like pious Jews—healed a crippled beggar and used the opportunity to preach Christ to the crowd. "The priests and the captain of the temple guard and the Sadducees came up to Peter and John while they were speaking to the people. They were greatly disturbed because the apostles were teaching the people and proclaiming in Jesus the resurrection of the dead" (Acts 4:1-2). Here is the point of contention that persists to this day. If Christ has not risen from the dead, then our faith is in vain. But if He has risen from the dead, then the faith of His opponents is in vain. Since Christ has risen from the dead, our good works inspired by faith lay up for us treasure in heaven. But for those who are not connected with Christ by faith, all their works avail them nothing. All of their prayers, alms, religious exercises—all is in vain. Lutheran theologian Francis Pieper once asked rhetorically how many religions there were in the world. A hundred? Twenty? His answer? Only two: the religion of the Law, which demands in a thousand different systems that people try to earn their salvation by works; and the religion of the Gospel, which demands nothing and instead offers the consolation of Jesus Christ to poor sinners who have been crushed by the Law. As manifested among the Jews in the time of the early Church, this implacable religion of the Law was bound to oppose the truth of the Gospel.

To this day, Jews center their religion upon ethics, upon right actions. This is commendable in itself and produces many fine Jewish neighbors and citizens. But even the Hebrew Scriptures show clearly that the righteous anger of God against sin cannot be satisfied by moral striving (Psalm 51; Isaiah 53). Only the sacrifice of Jesus Christ can satisfy the wrath of God and grant forgiveness of sins and salvation. Good works do not lead to salvation; salvation leads to good works.

This opposition to the Gospel extends to all other heresies as well. Once you take away the Gospel, only the Law remains. And where the preaching of the Law prevails, as Luther pointed out, men are driven to rebellion, hypocrisy, or despair.

Persecution from the Jews notwithstanding, the focus of evangelistic efforts in the early days was upon the Jews. Peter was the apostle to the circumcised, Paul to the uncircumcised. All of the apostles, and most of the early believers, were Jews. As yet there was no New Testament. The Hebrew Scriptures—more properly the Septuagint, the Greek translation of the Old Testament—were the Bible of the early Church. The book of Psalms was its hymnal. In this predominantly Jewish milieu arose the first true heresy to threaten the fledgling Church from within—that of the Judaizers. These false apostles taught that even though you believed in Christ, you still had to keep the Jewish ceremonial law. If you were a Gentile, it wasn't good enough to be saved by faith. You had to be circumcised, you had to obey the dietary proscriptions, you had to become as Jewish as possible. With the Hebrew Scriptures as a text, it was easy for a false teacher to make these arguments.

Even Peter succumbed to these blandishments until he was confronted by Paul. "When Peter came to Antioch, I opposed him to his face, because he was clearly in the wrong. Before certain men came from James, he used to eat with the Gentiles. But when they arrived, he began to draw back and separate himself from the Gentiles because he was afraid of those who belonged to the circumcision group" (Galatians 2:11-12). Paul realized that we are saved by faith alone, not by works, however well-meaning. He was therefore bound by conscience and Scripture to oppose even a pillar of the Church like Peter who was being seduced by this heresy.

Even today there are those in the Church who advocate adherence to Jewish law: dietary restrictions, Sabbath worship, even extreme measures like the stoning of sinners. Who can understand the seductive power of legalism? Every pastor knows intuitively that Moses is strong, but Christ is weak. When you thunder from the pulpit you become like a god, the pews fill up, offerings increase, the people become terrified like the Israelites at Mount Sinai, and some even feign obedience. But to point people to the cross is risky: Lives truly change, but so slowly and quietly that nobody notices, you might not make up that summer budget shortfall in time for Sunday school rally day, and your attendance statistics might not impress the denominational executives who are in a position to nominate you for promotion. Better to assume the Gospel, put it in the background, and concentrate on the deeper truths now being revealed on the front lines of the move of God in our time: discipleship, promise keeping, accountability, shepherding. Law.

From the Jewish roots of the Christian faith sprang another error: millennialism—that is, the expectation that the Messiah would in His lifetime or at His return inaugurate a universal kingdom of peace and prosperity on this earth. Jesus spoke plainly to the official representative of the duly constituted secular government: "My kingdom is not of this world" (John 18:36). That is, His kingdom was not primarily concerned with secular matters like meat and drink and the related enterprises of economics, government, and the military. His kingdom is primarily concerned with the things that the world cannot give— righteousness, peace, and joy. The righteousness of God comes by grace through faith in the atoning death and resurrection of Jesus

Christ; the peace that passes understanding is established by the cessation of hostilities with a just God; the joy of the Holy Spirit flows from knowing Christ and His free salvation. Jesus needed to make this point with Pilate because the Jews of that time, as today, were expecting their messiah to usher in a secular kingdom (in which the Jews, of course, would reign supreme). Pilate, like secular officials today, was on guard against any potential overthrow of the government he was responsible for. He feared an armed rebellion led by this Jewish king. So Jesus made it plain to Pilate that His disciples were not going to fight. Pilate had nothing to fear.

Yet he had everything to fear, for Christianity, like leaven, changes every element of the societies it enters. Old things pass away. Everything becomes new. Good government, a sound economy, universities, hospitals . . . these are merely the by-products of Christian civilization. They will pass away at the end of the world. But well should they issue from the Church, for God who made the heavens and the earth sent His Son, Jesus Christ, to redeem the body along with the soul. Christian citizens are properly concerned with secular matters. They can and should serve in the military, run for public office, labor in the fine arts. These by-products benefit all, like the rain that falls on the just and the unjust. But they are not the main focus of the kingdom of God. The kingdom of God is primarily concerned with spiritual things, secondarily with material things. The Twelve indicated as much when faced with the demands of their congregation's welfare program: "It would not be right for us to neglect the ministry of the word of God in order to wait on tables" (Acts 6:2). They had their priorities straight. They did not oppose the soup kitchen. They knew that taking care of the poor was a good ministry, something our Lord would approve of. But as ministers they knew that their primary responsibility was elsewhere: "[We] will give our attention to prayer and the ministry of the word" (Acts 6:4). That is, the apostles would focus on preaching and worship, not administration and "leadership."

Nevertheless, the glittering Jewish vision of a secular kingdom found its way into the young Church and has persisted. The ambitious mother of James and John certainly had something like this in mind when she asked Jesus to grant that her sons sit on His right and left in His kingdom. This concept must also be the background of the disciples' question to the resurrected Christ: "Lord, are you at this time going to restore the kingdom to Israel?" (Acts 1:6). The reason Jews to this day refuse to accept Jesus as Messiah is that He did not establish a glorious secular kingdom. In this context Jesus' reply is especially penetrating, and one that every Jew and Christian should ponder: "It is not for you to know the times or dates the Father has set by his own authority. But you will receive power when the Holy Spirit comes on you; and you will be my witnesses in Jerusalem, and in all Judea and Samaria, and to the ends of the earth" (Acts 1:7-8). That is, focus on the work of evangelism and not on millennial speculations. Has anyone heeded this admonition? The Montanists of the second century whipped up their followers to a fever pitch with millennialist preaching. The heresy revived around 400 when Rome was falling, again in 1000 at the turn of the first millennium, again and again in the sixteenth and nineteenth centuries, and continues to our own day. Of course the Second Coming of Christ is imminent. The Bible says so. It is an article of faith in the creeds. But Jesus Himself says that it should not be the main focus of our theology and practice.

Paganism

As Paul took the Gospel away from Jerusalem and into Europe, the faith began to encounter paganism. It is a curiosity of our language that the word *pagan* comes from the Latin for "country." Christianity in the beginning was an urban movement; the apostles went from town to town, and the churches were named after their cities: Jerusalem, Antioch, Rome, Corinth. Only later did the faith spread to the country. It was out in the farmlands that belief in the old gods persisted. So we know it was very early in the movement when Paul encountered the pagans in the great city of Athens. "He was greatly distressed to see that the city was full of idols. So he reasoned in the synagogue with the Jews and the God-fearing Greeks, as well as in the marketplace day by day with those who happened to be there. A group of Epicurean and Stoic philosophers began to dispute with him. Some of them asked, 'What is this babbler trying to say?' Others remarked, 'He seems to be advocating foreign gods.' They said this because Paul was preaching the good news about Jesus and the resurrection" (Acts 17:16-18). Paul was taking on all comers, Jewish and pagan alike. In the synagogue he argued from the Scriptures that Jesus was the Christ. In the *agora*, or marketplace, there was an area where learned men conversed and disputed. He told them the same thing he told the Jews: the blessed Gospel of Jesus Christ, centered in His glorious resurrection from the dead; that men no longer have to strive for salvation; that it is a free gift from the one true God who made heaven and earth.

Of course it seemed like nonsense to them at first. They were experts at reasoning, and one cannot arrive at a saving faith by a process of ratiocination. It is a matter of divine revelation. "Faith comes through hearing the message, and the message is heard through the word of Christ" (Romans 10:17). You preach the Word, the Holy Spirit works through the Word; some repent and believe, others turn away. So it was for Paul in Athens. "When they heard about the resurrection of the dead, some of them sneered, but others said, 'We want to hear you again on this subject'" (Acts 17:32). But from that time on, for better or for worse, the Christian faith that originated in the East was now connected with Western culture. The New Testament was written in a Western language, and Western thought-forms became the mode of discourse for the Church.

Inevitably, pagan influences crept into the Church. Greek religion centered in the cult of the ancient pantheon of gods and goddesses, with Zeus as the chief divinity along with his wife, Hera. These myths contain much human insight, and they can be studied profitably by good Christians. But as a working religion, mythology must be rejected. So it was that the preaching of Paul was gaining many adherents for Christianity in Ephesus. This city was known for the temple of Artemis (Diana), the virgin goddess of the hunt, associated with the moon and its precious metal, silver. "A silversmith named Demetrius, who made silver shrines of Artemis, brought in no little business for the craftsmen" (Acts 19:24). Here is the association of pagan religion and commerce, a natural connection for this-world religions. The pagans knew how to market their religion. The fledgling church in Ephesus was threatening not only the cult of Artemis but the economy as well. So Demetrius incited a riot. The mob seized Paul and his companions and rushed them to the public theater. There a chaotic scene ensued: "The assembly was in confusion: Some were shouting one thing, some another. Most of the people did not even know why they were there" (v. 32).

The pagans, like the Jews, were quick to realize what a threat this teaching of Christ was to their way of life and economic system. As the religions jostled with each other in the marketplace of ideas, some pagan influences penetrated and became incorporated into Christianity. In place of Diana/Artemis—or Juno/Hera or whichever goddess you chose, there was one or more in every pagan cult—there arose a veneration of Mary, mother of our Lord, a virgin, hence pure and blessed, therefore surely almost divine. Jesus Himself seems to warn against an incipient Mariolatry in the incident recorded in Luke: "A woman in the crowd called out, 'Blessed is the mother who gave you birth and nursed you.' He replied, 'Blessed rather are those who hear the word of God and obey it'" (11:27-28). This took place in Jerusalem, but don't forget that the city had been Hellenized since the conquest of Alexander the Great. Mary was indeed a great saint whose life of faith and obedience is worthy of honor and emulation along with Moses, Peter, and all saints. But she, like us, was only human. The point, as Jesus foresaw, is for us not to worship the saints but to follow their example by producing faith and good works in our own lives. In other words, be a saint yourself.

Gnosticism

A second pagan influence in the early Church was Gnosticism, so named from the Greek word for knowledge, *gnosis*. The Gnostic movement was pervasive in the Mediterranean world, certainly appealing to the Greek mind, perhaps originating in Persia and spreading West with the conquests of Alexander the Great (356-323 B.C.). The Gnostics held that certain special people—*pneumatikoi*—were endowed with special ability to comprehend esoteric divine mysteries. The focus on intellect and spirit led to a rejection of material things as inherently evil. God is a pure abstraction, totally other. In its focus on spiritual things at the expense of the material, the Gnostics represented a purely Ideational force in society. (Keep an eye on their ideas, for they crop up again and again throughout history, especially in the renewal of paganism in the twentieth century.) The Gnostics rejected the Christian doctrine of the incarnation of Christ, the idea that God became a man, born of woman. Jesus was for them a mere man who for a time had the divine spark. The Gnostics had women as priestesses, in reaction to which the custom arose of Christian pastors growing beards, so that a worshiper entering a public assembly could tell at a glance whether or not it was orthodox.

With matter being evil, Gnostic ethics split naturally in two directions, one toward asceticism, the other paradoxically but logically toward indulgence. The material world is evil, but as a Gnostic you are above material things. You prove this either by denying yourself all material pleasures and involvement or by wallowing in the pleasures of the flesh. The apostle John lived long enough to see the spread of Gnosticism begin to influence the fledgling Christian Church. A defense against the Gnostics forms the framework of much of his thought and springs forth in specific passages: "Dear friends, do not believe every spirit, but test the spirits to see whether they are from God, because many false prophets have gone out into the world. This is how you can recognize the Spirit of God: Every spirit that acknowledges that Jesus Christ has come in the flesh is from God, but every spirit that does not acknowledge Jesus is not from God. This is the spirit of the antichrist, which you have heard is coming and even now is already in the world" (1 John 4:1-3). John puts his finger on the central issue—as always, the Gospel in all its articles of belief. A prophet and a preacher are the same thing. There are true and false preachers. A true preacher will have the Spirit of God. This Spirit will acknowledge that Jesus is the Messiah, the Savior of the world, and that He came in the flesh, died in the flesh, rose in the flesh, ascended in the flesh, will return in the flesh, will raise all flesh from the dead, and will redeem the body along with the soul.

Gnosticism, like all heresies, never was completely eradicated. As long as the devil continues to operate, heresy will return in new guises. Gnosticism enjoyed another revival in the seventh and eighth centuries. Its spirit lives on today in superspiritual groups that subordinate the objective truth of Holy Scripture to human feelings and advocate a female priesthood.

John refers here to antichrist. Let me say plainly that the antichrist of Scripture is no comic-book archvillain such as we see in the popular apocalyptic novels and end-times books of our day. Writers with vivid imaginations concoct fanciful figures that rule the world like a Hitler with supernatural powers. In reality, the term is self-defining. The antichrist is any person, institution, office, or philosophy that opposes Christ. What opposes Christ? Anything that opposes the Gospel. The Gnostics opposed the Gospel with false teaching about Christ. The Bible says He was God's one and only Son, come in the flesh. The Gnostics said no—He was only a man, albeit with divine powers. The Church said that because Jesus was the Son of God, His death and resurrection brought salvation to all mankind as a free gift. The Gnostics said no—man is saved by inner illumination, by striving for enlightenment. In other words, inasmuch as knowledge is a product of the human will, by works. Nothing is more antichrist than this: turning poor sinners away from the grace of God to their own vain efforts. Note also that John said, "This *is* the spirit of the antichrist." He understood clearly—and so should we—that the entire time between the first and second comings of Christ is the end time during which antichrist operates. John expected Christ to return in His lifetime. So should we. John wasn't looking for some strange apparition to appear in the future. He was contending with antichrist in the present. So should we.

One more point. The Greek word *homologeo* in verse 2, which the NIV translates as "acknowledges," really means "say the same thing as" or "confess." That which is antichrist will not acknowledge or confess that Jesus Christ has come in the flesh. The idea here is that true Christianity is always distinguished by a confession, a doctrinal standard to which all adhere, and against which heresy is defined and rejected. In other words, creeds. Statements of belief. Dogma. We see the beginnings of confessionalism in phrases like "Jesus Christ is Lord" that are scattered throughout the New Testament. These are summaries of Bible doctrine. St. Paul writes in the earliest of all Christian Scriptures, "For what I received I passed on to you as of first importance: that Christ died for our sins according to the Scriptures, that he was buried, that he was raised on the third day according to the Scriptures" (1 Corinthians 15:3-4). One is struck by how similar this sounds to the second article of the Apostles' Creed. As Christianity spread and the attacks of heresy became more intense, it was perfectly natural for the Church to define orthodox belief by summarizing the true teaching of the Bible in creeds.

Toward the Nicene Creed

We have seen from the pages of the New Testament itself that there was no golden age in apostolic times. Fierce doctrinal battles raged within the Church. With the passing of the original apostles, the fledgling Church entered into an even more perilous time. Cults, sects, and false prophets proliferated, along with intensified physical persecution by the Roman government. A new Christian coming to a city in the Empire not only had to fear for his life—he also faced a situation as confusing as that of America today with its proliferation of denominations. There was a Gnostic church and an Arian church and a Marcionite church, not to mention the Nestorians and the Pelagians and the Apollinarians. All of them claimed that they alone interpreted the Bible correctly. Where was the true Church to be found? What were its marks? The mark of the true church was then what it always has been—the Holy Gospel; that is, the doctrine of justification by faith alone, expressed in every activity of the congregation: preaching, teaching, worship, and Sacraments.

Marcion (100-160) taught the love of God. So committed was he to the idea of a loving God, in fact, that he came to the conclusion that there were two gods in the Bible, one of love and another of wrath. To propagate his ideas, Marcion produced a special edition of the Bible with no Old Testament—there's too much in there about God's anger and divine judgment. He also cut out all of those uncomfortable parts in the New Testament where Jesus talked like a righteous judge. So Marcion was able to redefine Christianity as all Gospel and no Law. Needless to say, he became very popular.

The Monarchians arose during the second and third centuries. They focused on the idea of God as monarch or sovereign. In their theology, God was a single being who could not subdivide Himself or share His glory with another. Christ, therefore, was a man—perhaps a great moral philosopher, perhaps endued with supernatural power, but in the end not divine. In our day they might argue that Jesus never claimed to be the Son of God.

Like all heretics, they based their argument on Scripture—just not *all* of Scripture. That is the challenge of theology, to comprehend the whole Bible and keep the entire corpus of divine revelation in balance. It can be done. Why else would God have revealed His Word to us? But heretics are lazy as well as perverted and take shortcuts with their teaching.

Montanus flourished during this time, declaring himself the special instrument of the Spirit that had been promised by Christ. His followers, calling themselves Montanists, continued to cultivate extraordinary manifestations of the Spirit such as speaking in tongues long after the phenomenon had ceased with the apostolic age. In addition, their fanatical preoccupation with the immediate return of Christ led them to disengage with the world and lead ascetic lives.

There are always outside forces arrayed against Christ and His Church, physical as well as spiritual, but the devil concentrates on destroying the faith from the inside. A case in point is that of Apollinarius (310-390), who rose in the Church and became bishop of Laodicea. If the Monarchians made Christ more man and less God, the Apollinarians did the opposite. They made him more God and less man, teaching that Christ had no human soul, only the *logos* or eternal divine Word. In their view, Christ only appeared to have a human body. One can see the affinity with Gnosticism, a field of syncretistic religious thought that has kept reappearing throughout the Christian era. Of course if Christ did not truly have a human body, then there was no truly atoning sacrifice on the cross. It was only symbolic. The result of this teaching is that the poor sinner is never really sure if his sins are truly forgiven.

Then there was Arius (d. 336), a priest in Alexandria who almost destroyed the Church by touching off a controversy that raged for sixty years. His view was that God was above and beyond this world, a complete abstraction, a being totally other than the benighted human race. Because of his nature, the Arian god could not have been involved directly in the creation of this world. Therefore he created an intermediate being, the Logos, or Son, who was not eternal and not true God, but through whom the world was created. In time this Logos took on human flesh. He was not divine and not sinless, but he chose the good and taught morality. So here God is higher than the God of the Bible, and Christ is less than the Christ of the Bible. God is completely inaccessible, but Christ is a man we can identify with.

Arius was opposed by Athanasius (293-373), one of the great theologians and fathers of the early Church. The Apostles' Creed, with its Trinitarian structure, had long been in use as a catechism for new converts. The growing assent in the Church of the doctrine of the Trinity—that there was one God but three persons (Father, Son, and Holy Spirit)—was staunchly defended by Athanasius against the Arians. By this time Constantine (280-337) had become the first Christian emperor of Rome and convened a general council of church leaders in the city of Nicea in the year 325. The result was that under the leadership of Athanasius the orthodox party prevailed. The Nicene Creed was written as a standard and declaration of the true faith, affirming—specifically against the Arians—that the Lord Jesus Christ is "the only-begotten Son of God, begotten of his Father before all worlds, God of God, Light of Light, very God of very God, begotten, not made, being of one substance with the Father, by whom all things were made." The words "of one substance" were specifically included as a clause in the creed that the Arians could never possibly agree to.

Of course that wasn't the end of it. Arius continued to defend his views. Heretics never admit defeat. After Constantine died, Athanasius was banished twice for his defense of orthodoxy. It is said that his epitaph read, *Athanasius contra mundi* ("Athanasius against the world"). But the true faith had been defined for the ages; the true nature of Christ, both God and man, had been proclaimed.

Post-Nicene Heresies

Meanwhile, Manichaeism had been filtering into the Roman Empire. Mani (216-277), its Persian founder, had taught a basic religious dualism: There is not one supreme God over all creation, but rather two equal and opposing spiritual forces—one of darkness, the other of light. Sometimes the kingdom of light would prevail; then the empire of the dark side would strike back. And on and on the conflict would ensue, episode after episode. Eventually the world would end by fire. Jesus in this scheme was not true man nor suffering sacrifice. He was rather an agent of the light, one who is incapable of suffering, who came to teach men detachment from this world in a life of asceticism. It was an attractive religion to many, including one young philosophy student from North Africa.

Augustine (354-430), now known universally as "Saint," was a brilliant student but, like many students, susceptible to bad influences. At Carthage, where he had gone to study, he fell into a life of sexual promiscuity and at eighteen fathered an illegitimate child by his mistress. During this time he came to espouse the views of the Manichaeans for no less than nine years. Augustine's mother Monica was a devout Christian, however, and never ceased to pray for her son. Augustine eventually become a professor in Milan. There he met Bishop Ambrose, who taught him the Bible and the way of Christ. What young person cannot identify with Augustine's prayer during this period of spiritual struggle: "Lord, make me pure, but not yet." One of the most poignant passages in all of literature is in the *Confessions* where Augustine describes himself wrestling within his soul while visiting a friend's house. Left alone in the garden, he found an open Bible. Through its words, he found salvation. Augustine was baptized in 387 and became a pastor and bishop of the city of Hippo in his native North Africa. He was now a defender of the faith he once had rejected.

It was good for the faith to have such an able defender at such a critical time, for Augustine was contemporaneous with one of the most notable of all Christian heretics, Pelagius (360-420). Leaving his native Britain and coming to Rome around 400, Pelagius spread his teaching that man is saved not by faith but by works. Many of the early controversies were over Christology. The inroads of the heretics had forced the fathers to define the true nature of Christ. While so occupied, they had not yet reached consensus on the doctrine of justification. Like an army with its forces marshaled at the front, they were vulnerable from the flank. Here came Pelagius, teaching that man's nature since the Fall is not totally depraved. Man has free will. There is a spark of goodness in each of us, something attractive to God that makes us worthy of saving. We can choose the good; we can do things that please God and earn salvation. Augustine wrote *De natura et gratia* (*Of Nature and Grace*) specifically against the Pelagians. In this work he effectively defined the doctrine of justification by grace through faith in Jesus Christ—a theological concept that later grew weak in the Western church until rediscovered by Martin Luther.

On the basis of Augustine's defense of pure doctrine, Pope Innocent I condemned and excommunicated Pelagius. The heretical priest traveled east and eventually disappeared from history. But his ideas lived on, eventually being transformed into Semi-Pelagianism, the idea that man is saved by both faith and works. God does His part, and you do yours. God helps those who help themselves. Salvation is not by grace alone. You have to make a decision for Christ. Let the reader judge whether the ideas of Pelagius have been completely eradicated.

Meanwhile controversies about the person and nature of Christ had continued. Eutyches (378-454) asserted that there were not two natures in Christ but one. That is, Christ had been human and divine, but eventually the human nature was swallowed up by the divine, and Christ exists now in eternity only as a supernatural, spiritual being. From the Greek *mono* (single) and *physis* (nature), the term *Monophysite* came to describe the teachings of Eutyches.

In response to this heresy, a general council of the Church was held in 451 in Chalcedon, a city opposite Constantinople. Under the leadership of Leo the Great, bishop of Rome, this council articulated the orthodox belief that Christ was one person but of two distinct natures—human and divine—during His life on earth and will be for all eternity.

Unfortunately, the Eutychian or Monophysite heresy continued to sweep through the Eastern churches into the fifth and sixth centuries. The churches in Armenia, Syria, Palestine, Egypt, and North Africa persisted in heresy, resulting in a permanent schism that continues to this day. Church authorities, still allied with the state, cracked down on the schismatics. So severe was the antagonism with Constantinople that the Monophysite Christians actually welcomed the more tolerant administrative policies and lower taxes of a new religion that was rapidly spreading out of Arabia: Islam.

5

Islam

The Ideational phase of civilization that emerged in the West after the fall of Sensate Rome was decidedly spiritual in its preoccupations. But Christianity was not the only system of religious thought. Pagan thought challenged the faith, as did new heretical spirituality from within. A new Ideational system of spirituality arose in Arabia in the seventh century: Islam. If Christianity at its best maintains a balance between Ideational and Sensate elements, Islam, it will be seen, is more purely Ideational. And in the new Ideational era emerging in the West today, it is perhaps not surprising to find that Islam has once again become a major competitor to Christianity.

"Islam," C. S. Lewis remarked, "is only the greatest of the Christian heresies" (102). Why he should have said that is a matter worth exploring. There is a bit of truth to the statement, though it is not entirely accurate. Narrowly defined, heresy is authentic only if it arises from within the Church. Arius, who essentially denied the divinity of Christ, was a prominent bishop in the early Church. Pelagius, who taught salvation by works and not by faith, was a monk. These classic heresies originated inside the Church. Islam did not. It sprang up out of the world of seventh-century Arabian polytheism. It came from outside the Church. So in this sense, it is not a true heresy.

Yet in another sense, Lewis is entirely right. In terms of the *ideas* of Islam, it must be ranked as a Christian heresy since everything about it springs from the wider Christian context and undermines and attacks it with false theology. Islam teaches that there is one God, which Christianity also teaches. But it denies that Jesus is the divine Son of God. Islam teaches that we must repent and submit to the one God, which Christianity also teaches. But it asserts that a man can be saved by external obedience to the works of the Law. In a way, Islam is a kind of Christianity reduced to the first article of the Apostles' Creed: "I believe in God the Father almighty, maker of heaven and earth." In orthodox Christianity, the first article speaks of the Father-Creator. The second article defines the Son-Redeemer, the third article the Holy Spirit-Sanctifier. If the first article is all you admit, then a religion inevitably arises that is radically monotheistic and radically legalistic. And that is exactly what we have in Islam.

Origins of Islam

In a way, one is forced to admit that Islam has the advantage over Christianity in certain aspects. From time to time, scholars embark on a quest for the historical Jesus—that is, they exclude *a priori* the evidence of the Bible and try to establish a "real" Jesus from other, non-biblical, non-devotional sources. Of course they never find him. Christ, like the Holy Grail, can be found only by the pure of heart. That is, by penitent sinners. But the scholars keep trying.

With Muhammad, the founder of Islam, this problem does not exist. His life abounds in the kind of eyewitness detail that historians love: He was short of stature but walked fast everywhere he went. His hair and beard were reddish. He liked women and fast horses and camels. His hobby was cobbling shoes, and the first thing he did when he came home was use a toothpick. He died in the year 632 in Medina, Arabia, and everyone knows the location of his grave. No one ever goes on a search for the historical Muhammad.

It is in this richly historic context that Islam arises from a historic

Muhammad. He was born in Mecca, Arabia, in A.D. 570 and was orphaned at a young age. Taken in by relatives, he lived a rather knockabout existence until a wealthy widow recognized his potential and gave him a position as a merchant in her company. Muhammad was successful in business for fifteen years and eventually married his benefactress. Given to religious contemplation, Muhammad at forty began to seek the solitude of the caves around Mecca. There, in 610, on the "night of power," he supposedly saw the angel Gabriel and was given the first of his prophetic revelations.

This gives Islam a second advantage over Christianity. All the revelation was given to one man in one lifetime. There it all is in the Qur'an, neat as can be. Islamic revelation is not spread out over the centuries in a sprawling, multi-authored library like we have in the Bible. Hence Islam never has to worry about anything like the modern, liberal, historical-critical method of scholarship that has done so much to undermine the authority of the Bible in the West.

Arabia in the seventh century was not a true nation, but a region seething with warring tribes and factions. Likewise, it was mostly polytheistic in religion. There was in Arabia neither political nor spiritual unity. The Arabs are proud to trace their lineage to Abraham through Ishmael. But unlike Abraham they did not worship the one true God who made heaven and earth. The religion of the Arabs centered in the city of Mecca, and in the temple there were shrines to many gods. The holiest place was the Kaaba, a very ancient cube-shaped building that, according to tradition, was built by Abraham and Ishmael. In the wall of the Kaaba was set the Black Stone supposedly given to Abraham by Gabriel. There was some native monotheism of a primitive sort, particularly in Medina, but the Arabs for the most part worshiped many gods.

At the same time there were other religious influences in the area. The Jews constituted a strong presence on the Arabian peninsula and exerted a significant influence on Arabic culture and ideas. The Christians were a weak presence, and those who were there had been rent by centuries of theological division. In addition, by the seventh century the Eastern Christian Empire (the Roman Empire had come to an end in 476) was stressed and weakened from long wars of attrition with the rival Persian empire. The armies of both had fought to an exhausted stalemate, resulting in a power vacuum not unlike that which had occurred centuries earlier between Assyria and Egypt, during which the kingdom of David had arisen. Recall too that the predominantly Monophysite churches of the area had been persecuted by Constantinople.

Into this milieu came Muhammad, seeking God in his cave outside Mecca. There he claims to have had a vision of the angel Gabriel, who gave him words of divine revelation to relate to the people. These prophetic utterances were passed on by oral tradition—phenomenal powers of memory were common among ancient peoples—and later collected and written down by Muhammad's personal secretary in the Qur'an, the holy book of Islam. The word *Qur'an* means, "recite." Rote recitation of the holy words of the prophet is esteemed most highly among Muslims, even more highly than preaching and theology. Recall the dramatic scene in the film *Lawrence of Arabia* when Prince Faisal and his servant and their friend are all three contentedly reciting the Qur'an to each other late in the evening in their tent. As they pause for a moment's reflection, Lawrence recites the next line to the astonishment of all.

Islamic Doctrine

Esteem for Muhammad as a prophet of God is foundational to all of Islam. Muhammad claimed—and Muslims affirm—that there were many prophets who went before. Many are familiar to us—Abraham and Moses from the Old Testament, Jesus from the New. Jesus was called "the Word of God" by the Muslims, just as He was by the Gnostics. Muslims hold that Jesus did not die on the cross to take away our sins—His disciples managed an escape for Him somehow—

and certainly He never rose from the dead. He was a good and great man and a prophet, but not the Son of God. Nor was Muhammad the Son of God. There is no Son of God. There is only Allah. But Muhammad was the last and greatest prophet, who delivered the final revelation of God to mankind. All who went before gave partial revelations, but Muhammad's was the ultimate and last word from heaven.

Luther called this "sheer enthusiasm." By this he did not mean the kind of excitement we feel in St. Louis when the Cardinals are winning. Luther meant something far more serious. *Enthusiasm* as a theological term is derived from the Greek words *en* ("in") plus *theos* ("God"). It conveys the idea of God being in you to such an extent that you become inspired and get special, direct revelations from Him apart from the divinely inspired Word of God in the Bible. In a word, fanaticism.

Of course this enthusiasm or fanaticism was, has been, and always will be in the Church. The devil stirs it up. So fanaticism provides another sense in which Islam can be seen as a Christian heresy. The aforementioned Montanus taught that the charismatic gifts, such as speaking in tongues, did not expire with the apostles. He held that there was to be ongoing revelation from God in the Church. It didn't stop with Christ and the apostles. We are not to be limited to the written Word of God. In fact, Montanus himself claimed to be the promised *Paraclete* of John's Gospel—the Holy Comforter whom Christ would send to lead the Church into all truth. Naturally Montanus succeeded in gathering a large following and drawing many away from the true faith. The simple are always impressed by dynamic preachers, whether they are preaching the truth or not. And Montanus was not.

Whenever a man sets himself up as a prophet and claims to have received a new word from God, one thing and only one results: more law. The Gospel is like Jesus. It is humble and lowly; it is patient and kind; it does not raise its voice; it is content to receive from God; it is willing to suffer. The Law is like Muhammad. It is dynamic and powerful; it is aggressive and masterful; it is overwhelming and swift; it is directive and positive. And it is willing to kill. In Luther's day a fanatic named Carlstadt was doing the same thing as Montanus and Muhammad had done in ancient times. In our own day others continue this heretical tradition.

But of course it is never advertised as tradition. It is always promoted as something new from the Lord, something that puts you on the front lines of the moving of God in our age. Or so it is claimed. In reality, it is the vanity of a man's imagination, thinking that the ideas buzzing around in his head are divine revelation when they are only his own thoughts or, worse yet, the influence of an evil spirit disguising itself as an angel of light. Luther spoke derisively of these prophets as *Schwärmer*, from the German word for "swarm." You get the picture. Enthusiasm is the wind and the fire and the earthquake. True revelation is the still, small voice.

And so we see Muhammad, middle-aged and restless, sitting and contemplating in a cave outside of Mecca. He claims to have seen the angel Gabriel. He claims to have received a final revelation from God for the world. He claims to be the last and greatest prophet, sent by God to enlighten the human race. And what was the result? More law.

Yet this legalism is the thing about Islam that in a way gives it yet another advantage over the Christian faith: It is eminently doable. It teaches salvation by works, and in so doing demands only a few simple works that any average person can accomplish. As Roland Miller points out, "Islam is geared to the natural capacity of humans and does not require more than is achievable" (119). You pray toward Mecca five times a day. You go to the mosque once a week. You acknowledge Allah as the one God and Muhammad as his prophet. Ask any Muslim if he were to die tonight and stand before God and be asked, "Why should I let you into my heaven?" and he will be able to answer in all truthfulness and with the full assent of his religion, "Because I've been a good person and have tried to obey God's Law."

The word *Islam* means "submission," and a Muslim is "one who submits" to the rule of Allah in obedience to his laws.

Central to Muhammad's teaching is radical monotheism, something very different from the prevalent polytheism of Arabia in his day. It is known that Muhammad had contact with Jewish rabbis and Christian monks in the area. Perhaps that is where he gained some of his ideas. In his theology, however, there is no room for the doctrine of the Holy Trinity. Jesus was a prophet but not the Son of God, and not the Savior of the world. In this way Muhammad reflects the ideas of heretical Christian theology prevalent in the seventh century and takes them radically further into falsehood.

Muhammad's teaching, as contained in the Qur'an, forbids usury (which is why a sheik must deposit his money in a Swiss bank; Arabian banks don't give or charge interest), gambling (unless you are visiting Monaco), the drinking of alcohol (at least on Islamic soil), and the eating of pork (in Muslim eschatology, at the end of the world Jesus will return to kill all the pigs). It demands a strict eye-for-an-eye justice: Thieves must have a hand cut off; women who commit adultery are to be publicly beheaded. Slavery is permitted (much of the African slave trade was generated by Muslim slavers working the interior of Africa; slaves who were taken east were never heard from again). A man may have up to four wives, as long as he can adequately provide for them (a revelation to many an American girl who married a Muslim only to find that he already had other wives). One is to give honor to parents, show kindness to slaves and wives, give alms to the poor, and work hard. Fasting is required during Ramadan, the ninth month of the Muslim calendar; one is to take no food or drink from dawn to sunset, after which a meal may be consumed. For those who can afford it and are physically able, the *Hajj* or "pilgrimage" to Mecca is required. Both good and bad deeds are recorded by angels and will be rewarded accordingly both in this life and in eternity. As in Christianity and Pharisaic Judaism, there will be a resurrection and last judgment. Muslim heaven is described with material details, including beautiful gardens, luscious fruits, plenty of wine, uphol-stered couches, and girls, girls, girls.

So Islam is concerned more with *orthopraxy* (right practice) than *orthodoxy* (right belief). The energies of Muslim communities are focused on building a better world in the here and now and helping people cope with their practical, day-to-day problems. The sermons of Muslim *imams* focus on the felt needs of ordinary people. Muslims feel a special connection with each other in the local mosque and a real brotherly kinship with fellow believers around the world. Amidst the hustle and bustle of the modern world, they somehow manage to per-petuate traditional family values. Children are highly esteemed. Women are taught to keep their place. Men are shown how to pro-vide well and care for their families. No wonder Islam is growing rapidly in the United States today, especially among black people in urban areas. It solves practical problems.

Problems in Islamic Theology

Even so, theological problems crop up in Islam, most of them stem-ming from the first premise of Islam, that there is no God but Allah. Foremost of these is the problem of predestination. If there is one supreme Being who created the universe and rules over all things, then He must be all-powerful and all-knowing. Hence He knows every-thing that is going to happen, and since He knows everything that is going to happen, everything He knows must inevitably come to pass by His divine foreknowledge and eternal decree. Truly, Allah is great. In fact, Allah is so great in this context that man is nothing. He has no free will at all and is reduced to a mere puppet. Muslim theology attempts to solve this problem by moving Allah upstairs—that is, to consign His omnipotence to the realm of general, universal, and nat-ural law, so as to leave room for human free will and action in this world below.

As soon as this is done, however, another problem emerges. God becomes what Reformed theologian Karl Barth called *totaliter aliter* (totally other). That is, He is completely of a different nature and mind than that of human beings, and He cannot be known at all as He is in His essential being. He is remote, detached, a God who is unapproachable, who cannot be known, with whom one cannot have a personal relationship.

Given the initial fanaticism of Muhammad himself, it was inevitable that an enthusiastic sect would emerge in Islam precisely at the point of this problem. This was *Sufism*, a sect devoted to ascetic practices and long periods of meditation and spiritual exercises designed to bring one into mystical communion with Allah during this earthly life. Of course not every Muslim could be a *sufi*, in the same way that not every Christian could be a monk.

This was the intractable problem facing Imam al-Ghazali (1058-1111), widely considered to be the greatest Muslim theologian. A brilliant young student and thinker, he was appointed chief expert in Islamic law in Baghdad at age thirty-three, only to become disenchanted by the dryness and legalism of Islamic philosophy and theology. Duress of mind led to physical illness, whereupon al-Ghazali left his position and began to travel, ending up meditating long hours in a corner of the mosque in Damascus. He emerged with a kind of harmony between orthodoxy and mysticism: Allah is loving and wants a relationship with men; so men must use some of the spiritual disciplines of Sufism to attain a personal experience of Allah, then go back to traditional Islamic practice, but now doing good works from the heart instead of mere external obedience to the Law.

One must sigh with regret that al-Ghazali's footsteps did not lead him down the Street Called Straight in Damascus and into the Christian church that has been there since the time of St. Paul. There he might have learned the true solution to his theological problem. In Christ, your personal relationship with a loving God comes at the beginning. And this is not by works, but rather by grace through faith. Once this relationship is established by faith, sealed in Baptism, and nourished by Holy Communion, good works naturally follow as a fruit of the Holy Spirit. It is a life based on the Gospel, not upon the Law.

In this regard, the problem of predestination can be solved with relative ease. In the Qur'an, there is only Law and no Gospel. In the Bible, there is both Law and Gospel. In Islam, the central premise of one supreme universal deity ruling over all things and all people must inevitably lead to a mechanical view of predestination. It cannot be otherwise without taking something away from Allah. In Christianity, however, we see that predestination is a doctrine of the Gospel but not of the Law. It is there for the comfort of persecuted, afflicted, and suffering Christians, to give them the assurance that their destiny is with Christ no matter how bad things get in this world. God has chosen them, elected them, predestined them for Himself from before the foundation of the world. It is God's will that all be saved and come to a knowledge of the truth (1 Timothy 2:4). Those who are saved must give the glory to God alone; those who are lost are entirely at fault in themselves. And as for human action, of course we have a measure of free will in the arena of civil affairs: what kind of car to buy, whom to vote for, whether or not to marry. But in the matter of salvation the sinner is bound to sin, no matter how agreeable his works may appear to the world. Without faith it is impossible to please God. In Christ, however, all we do by faith is pleasing to God, no matter how imperfect. He that is in us is greater than he that is in the world. Our compulsion to righteousness is more powerful than our compulsion to sin.

Progress of Islam

Theological problems aside—and all religions have them—Islam caught on rapidly and spread widely, becoming the second-largest world religion and having over a billion adherents today. Having received the first of his revelations from Allah, Muhammad went back into his native city and began to preach. This businessman-turned-prophet met with scorn, failure, and persecution, especially since he was criticizing the traditional way of life and the worship of many gods that had prevailed in Arabia since ancient times.

For twelve years he labored with limited success, gathering a small but devoted following. During this time Muhammad was well-treated by the Christians, especially when a persecuted group fled temporarily to Ethiopia for refuge. Accordingly, Christians and Jews—unlike idolaters—were given special status in Islamic realms as "people of the Book." At least as long as they toed the line.

But eventually persecution against Muhammad and his followers got so bad that they fled to the city of Medina, 250 miles north of Mecca. This escape, known ever after as the *Hejira*, was to mark the turning point in the fortunes of Islam. In fact, the Muslim calendar marks its beginning from this event in A.D. 622 The city of Medina was traditionally more open to monotheism among the Arabs and also had a large Jewish population. Not a pilgrimage city like Mecca, Medina was seriously divided politically by rival tribal factions and needed leadership. Muhammad was welcomed with open arms, and he quickly set about to reorganize the town according to the principles of his revelation.

Within a short period of time he gained so many new converts that he went from persecuted prophet to successful leader. He labored on a new city constitution. Since the first principle of Islam was one sovereign and supreme Allah, there was no intrinsic conflict between religion and government—yet another advantage of Islam. In Christianity the function of government has traditionally been seen as the administration of temporal justice. The function of the Church is the administration of God's grace. This is often described as the distinction between the kingdom of God's left hand and the kingdom of God's right hand. In His left hand, God holds the sword (government); in His right hand, God holds the chalice (Church). This flows out of the classic distinction between Law and Gospel in Scripture. But in Islam there is no Gospel. God holds a sword in each hand. There is no wall of separation between religion and state. So Muhammad set up a theocracy with himself at the top of the administrative flow chart.

Naturally the constitution was based on Islamic principles. Refugees and immigrants and the poor were to be provided for from a fund created by levying 20 percent of war booty. Jews were granted official tolerance, at least in theory. Some of the rabbis in Medina were hostile to Muhammad and drew his disapproval. After a dispute, two tribes were expelled from the city. As for a third tribe, when its members undermined the defense of the city during a battle, Muhammad had the men beheaded and the women and children sold into slavery.

Essential to the teachings of Muhammad—and key to the spread of Islam—was the concept of *jihad*. Usually translated "holy war," the term actually means "exertion" or "striving" against evil. The higher jihad is spiritual, the striving of the individual against sin. The lesser jihad, and the one usually associated with the term, is military action for the spread of Islam. The prophet was himself a warrior of exceptional skill and courage, able to motivate his troops and succeed in battle against heavy odds. In Arabian culture such virtues were highly esteemed. Not surprisingly, Islam promises great reward and immediate entrance into paradise for men killed in battle for the faith.

In 624, the Battle of Badr, near Medina, marked a turning point in the fortunes of Islam. Muhammad's army had gone out to raid a caravan from Mecca. The Meccans responded by sending a superior force in defense of the caravan. The two armies met at Badr—Muhammad with 300 men against a Meccan army of 900. Amazingly—miraculously, Muslims would say—Muhammad won the battle. It was the first of many military victories to come. With the rapid growth of the religion, Muhammad was finally able to return to Mecca with 10,000 followers in 630. He destroyed the idols in the temple but himself worshiped Allah at the Black Stone of the Kaaba, thus retaining an important link with Arab traditional religion. Mecca submitted to Islam and became the first of the religion's three holy cities (the others being Medina and Jerusalem).

Then, in 632, Muhammad died unexpectedly in Medina after a brief illness. He left no chosen successor, inadvertently creating a power vacuum that has divided Islam to this day. The largest sect of Islam is that of the Sunni, who believe that religious leaders should come from the descendants of Muhammad or his tribe. The second-largest group, the Shiites, believe that the chief leaders should come from descendants of Ali, Muhammad's son-in-law. Of the first four caliphs who succeeded Muhammad, three were assassinated. (The term *assassin* actually comes from later Islam. It is derived from the word *hashish* and came to describe men who would smoke dope and then go out and kill someone for Allah.)

Nevertheless Islam continued to expand by means of military prowess, trade, peace treaties, skill at negotiation, immigration, and strategic marriage. The Monophysite Christians welcomed their Muslim conquerors initially. Their taxes were lower and their policies more tolerant. Besides, in many ways Islam, with its lower view of Christ, was similar to their own religion. Jerusalem welcomed Uthman, the third caliph, in 638. Finding the old temple area on Mt. Moriah deserted, he cleared away some rubble and made himself a simple mosque—the beginning of what was to become the present-day Dome of the Rock.

In time, Muslim conquerors took the faith and civilization from Spain in the West to India and beyond in the East. Today, in fact, most Muslims live in Asia, not the Middle East. The Muslims would have conquered Europe at the beginning of what was to become the Middle Ages, but were defeated at the Battle of Poitiers (or Tours) by Charles Martel, "the Hammer," in 732, and so turned back to Spain. Still, Muslim ambition centered on the Christian West, especially after the depredations of the eight Crusades (1096-1277) that tried to reclaim the Holy Land for Christianity by military means. The Eastern Christian Roman Empire continued to weaken, even though the "millet" system of government under the Ottoman Turks (so admired by Toynbee) allowed Christian enclaves a measure of autonomy. Finally,

in 1453 Constantinople fell to Muslim forces. The city had a magnificent system of fortifications, but not enough men-at-arms to use them
effectively. The Turks entered the city, slaughtered its inhabitants, and
converted the magnificent Church of the Hagia Sophia ("holy wisdom") into a mosque.

From there it was a straight run up the Danube and into the heart
of Europe. The Turks advanced rapidly, killing all Christian war
refugees. They surrounded Vienna and laid siege in 1529. This military threat forced Holy Roman Emperor Charles V to deploy forces
that otherwise might have been used to stamp out the nascent
Protestant Reformation that had begun with Luther's Ninety-five
Theses in 1517. One thing after another went wrong for the Turkish
invaders, and they withdrew after a sudden snowstorm ended a miserable autumn campaign. Looters from Vienna went out to poke
around in the abandoned Turkish tents and found some sacks of funny
little brown beans. They tasted nasty and bitter but if boiled made a
pleasant and stimulating beverage. Especially with a little cream and
sugar. Thus entered Western civilization a substance without which no
subsequent military campaign—or church function, for that matter—
would ever have succeeded: coffee.

Decline and Revival

For a time, during the period of European ascendancy in world affairs
beginning in the sixteenth century, Islamic civilization fell into disarray. Many of the historic strongholds of Islam—Arabia, for instance,
and India—came under the dominance of foreign colonial powers.
Still, at its height the Muslim world built magnificent civilizations and
contributed many things to Western culture. For one thing, we all use
Arabic numerals. For another, Muslim philosophers preserved and
studied many texts of the ancient Greek writers—Plato and Aristotle
in particular—that might otherwise have been lost after the collapse
of Rome. These are the writings that came to have such decisive influ-

ence on the Renaissance and its rediscovery of classical literature. Anyone who has visited the Alhambra in Spain knows the grandeur of Islamic architecture. And medicine in Muslim lands was far more advanced than in Europe during the Middle Ages.

In recent centuries, especially since the development of the Middle Eastern oil business in the twentieth century, wealth has flowed into the Arabian peninsula, and with it, increased political power for Islam. Some of this has gone into improving the standard of living for the people. Some of it has gone into enhancing Islam. The spectacle of a resurgent Shiite Islam in Iran and the return of the Ayatollah Khomeini in the 1970s made a deep impression on all Americans. In Islam, religion and politics have always gone together, and "shadowy" terrorist organizations began to appear, bombing airports and taking hostages at the Olympic Games. In the 1990s in Iraq, dictator Saddam Hussein started the brief Gulf War by invading Kuwait, a neighboring Muslim state. Of course, one state in the Middle East is *not* Muslim, to the antagonism of all the rest: Israel. Continual sabre-rattling goes on, with Muslim politicians vowing to exterminate Israel, a country that was created by British colonialism. As I write, yet another Israeli-Palestinian peace accord has broken down. And so it will continue.

In fairness, it must be noted that the mainstream of Islam is moderate in tone. The terrorist groups are an anomaly, just as in America the murdering of abortionists by Christian gunmen is not representative of the religion as a whole.

Also, to digress briefly, Israel is a wholly secular state that contains some religious Jews. It has no pretensions of being or ever becoming a theocracy with the reinstitution of temple worship and sacrifice. One can argue on humanitarian grounds that the Jews after such a long *diaspora* should have a home of their own once again. But one cannot make such a claim on the basis of Scripture. The Old Testament prophecies that refer to the Jews returning to their homeland and rebuilding the temple were fulfilled in the repatriation that took place after the Babylonian captivity under the leadership of Ezra and Nehemiah. So the tensions between Muslim and Jew in the Middle East will continue. To complicate matters further, many Palestinians are traditionally Christian, and have been so since the time of the apostles, as have many Christian enclaves and congregations in Muslim territories such as Damascus and Baghdad. Bethlehem is predominantly Christian, and the believers there are sadly persecuted by the Jews.

Overall, then, we have today a resurgent Islam worldwide, a religion that began by gaining a following in Christian lands. It continues to advance rapidly, particularly in the United States. We find in Islam a religion that emphasizes the sovereignty of Allah, man's obedience and submission to him, a solid doctrine of predestination, practical preaching that addresses the problems of day-to-day living, and a stimulating vision of bringing divine precepts into the arena of public affairs. The same could be said of some Christian denominations today. No wonder Islam is on the upswing. It's just close enough to Christianity to lead many astray. All that's missing is the Gospel.

6

The Middle Ages

We have dwelt at some length on the theological development of the early Church. There were many ideas that opposed or undermined the Gospel—heresies that swarmed around the baby Church like horseflies in a manger. It is important to have a firm grasp of these ideas that have opposed the Gospel in the past, though. For as the Gospel continues its inexorable progress through the world, spreading like a good plague, these ideas will continue to be injected into the Church like an antidote from hell. More importantly for us at this critical juncture of history, we will probably see them come around again in a new Ideational phase of Western culture. The ascendancy of the Church in the West coincided—according to God's sovereign decree, we think—with the rise of an Ideational cultural dynamic, producing a Christianity that may have been overly spiritual. It will be seen later what an Ideational cultural dynamic looks like in a post-Christian society.

The Papacy

One of the impediments to the Gospel that arose during the nascent Middle Ages was the idea of Christianity investing supreme temporal ecclesiastical authority in one spiritual father—a pope. As noted, Christianity was at first an urban movement. Beginning at Jerusalem, the faith was spread by missionaries to the major population centers: Alexandria, Antioch, Corinth, Rome. In each city there was a bishop or overseer, a chief pastor who was responsible for the supervision of doctrine, worship, and ecclesiastical life. By common consent this arrangement worked satisfactorily, especially as a defense against the many heresies that were threatening the early Church. Bishops of the chief cities were among the dignitaries assembled by the emperor Constantine at the ecumenical Council of Nicea (325) in the controversy with the Arians.

As Christianity gained in strength and numbers, the bishop of Rome assumed more importance, first because of his seat in the ancient imperial city, and second because of his traditional association with Peter as first bishop there. Peter certainly had been at Rome. There he was closely associated with a gifted young disciple named John Mark—the same Mark who wrote the first Gospel based on Peter's firsthand accounts. In time the bishop of Rome came to be seen as *primus inter pares* ("first among equals") and was later called *pope* after the Latin *papa* ("father").

Certainly there had been outstanding Christian leaders among the early popes. For sheer personal courage, few excel Leo I, who walked alone out of the city in 452 and personally persuaded Attila the Hun to spare Rome. Gregory I, "The Great" (540-604), upheld the teaching of Augustine on justification by faith. To him is attributed the Gregorian chant, the ethereally beautiful music that so perfectly expresses the mystery of salvation. In the ninth century Hadrian I vigorously defended the orthodox faith against a revival of adoptionism—the false teaching that Jesus was born an ordinary human and was later "adopted" as the Son of God.

For a long time the bishops of Rome and Constantinople could justly claim equal preeminence. The historic seat of the Empire had been in Rome; the actual seat was in Constantinople from 326 on. Then the fall of the western Roman empire in the fifth century created a political vacuum in which opportunistic popes began to arrogate more and more power to themselves. In time the rising force of Islam in the East during the seventh and eighth centuries permanently diminished the power and prestige of Constantinople.

A powerful alliance between church and state developed with the coronation of Charlemagne (an enormous German warrior whose actual name was Karl der Grosse) as the first Holy Roman Emperor on December 25, 800. As previously noted, each *kairos* seems to have a symbolic event that marks it, and the coronation of Charlemagne can stand as symbolic of the beginning of the Middle Ages (see Figure 2, p. 48). The head of the newly-minted Christian version of the Roman Empire (here's that millennial vision of a kingdom of God on earth again) was crowned by Pope Leo III. So was laid the foundation for popes to claim supremacy not only over all Christendom but over all secular authority as well. What had begun as a benign ecclesiastical arrangement was now carried to its logical extremity.

By the time of Gregory VII (1020-1085) (known equally by his proper name, Hildebrand), papal power over the state had reached its zenith. A political dispute led the pope to excommunicate the Holy Roman Emperor, Henry IV. The emperor finally traveled to the pope's winter quarters at Canossa and stood outside barefoot in the snow begging for absolution. While subsequent political developments curtailed the pope's actual political power, it should be noted that the Vatican has never renounced the pope's claim to secular dominion. Indeed, theologian Hermann Sasse could declare in 1950, "It is no exaggeration to say that today the Vatican, next to Moscow and Washington, is one of the great centers of world politics."

For many Protestants it is an article of faith that the pope is the antichrist. This is to say that the papacy—even if this or that occupant of the throne seems a decent Christian man—is in and of itself an institution that works against Christ and opposes the Gospel. This was certainly evident when Pope Leo X excommunicated Martin Luther in 1521 for no other reason than that the young Augustinian friar was teaching justification by faith. Later in the sixteenth century the

Council of Trent, held under papal auspices, responded to the Reformation by declaring the doctrine of justification by faith anathema and affirming as official Roman Catholic dogma that man is saved by works (remember Pelagius?).

In 1999 representatives of the more theologically liberal and ecumenically-minded Lutheran church bodies believed they had overcome their differences with Rome over this matter and signed the Joint Declaration on the Doctrine of Justification. Then they were all embarrassed and dismayed when Pope John Paul II turned right around a few months later and issued a brand-new set of indulgences—that essential symbol of works-righteousness—for the Jubilee Year 2000. In truth, Rome yielded nothing in the Joint Declaration. Salvation by works is still the cornerstone of Roman Catholic theology. It was the Lutherans who sold out.

The secular authority of the pope had waned by the late Middle Ages, and the Reformation curtailed his spiritual hegemony. However, the papacy gradually began to recoup. At the First Vatican Council in 1870 the widely-held belief in papal infallibility was officially ratified as Catholic doctrine. This means two things. One: When the pope speaks *ex cathedra*—that is, makes a formal proclamation of church dogma "from the throne"—it is absolutely true and binding on the consciences of all Christians. Two: To be saved, you must believe that the pope is infallible.

The world had to wait eighty years for such an *ex cathedra* pronouncement, but it finally came in 1950 when Pope Pius XII officially declared—to the horror of all thinking Protestants—that the Virgin Mary was taken bodily up into heaven. There is, of course, not one syllable about this supposed Assumption of Mary in Scripture, but since when is an infallible pope bound by Scripture? What is also disturbing about this 1950 decree is that the encoded paganism of Mariolatry that had grown from the time of the early Church through the Middle Ages was now officially sanctioned by the modern Roman Catholic Church. It is now only a short step for a pope of the future to declare as official doctrine what is currently a widely-held belief: Mary as co-redemptrix. That is, Mary is our Redeemer equal to and along with Christ, and one must approach God through her. This is crass idolatry, and its proclamation would put the Roman Catholic Church outside the border of Christendom. At that point, so to speak, Luther would have to excommunicate the pope.

I hasten to add, however, that for all the error embedded in Rome, one cannot say categorically that Catholics aren't saved. The Gospel is preached there, even if tinged with legalism, and their Sacraments are valid, even if the Lord's Supper is misunderstood as something the priest offers to God. Besides, who are we Protestants to point the finger? It will be obvious to the perceptive reader that while I have refrained from singling out any particular denomination for criticism except my own, all of the aforementioned heresies are present to some degree somewhere in Protestantism today.

An Ideational Period

Seeing the alliance between church and state under the popes during the Middle Ages, one might argue that the period was more Sensate than Ideational, more interested in material things than spiritual things. To this I would reply that during the Middle Ages the state was viewed as being subordinate to or at least supportive of religion. In the Roman Empire, religion was subordinate to the state. The state was the supreme authority, and religion was to keep its place and encourage the populace in loyalty to the state. Caesar worship was not real religion, nor was Caesar seen as a real god in the same league with Jupiter and Apollo. Caesar worship was a mere formality of civil religion. Nobody took it all that seriously. Except the Christians, of course, who paid the price for their refusal to make even token obeisance to Caesar. Their sin was not so much real idolatry as perceived disloyalty. They put religion above the state. And, carried to its logical but evil extreme, that was to be the sin of the medieval popes.

So I here defend the proposition of seeing the Middle Ages, from about the eighth to the thirteenth century, as Ideational. As with the Dark Ages, the commonly-accepted nomenclature indicates a modern, Sensate point-of-view. People in the Middle Ages certainly did not think of their era as being sandwiched in between two, more importantly materialistic epochs of Western culture. Their present was as up-to-date to them as ours is to us.

In terms of cultural values, their focus was not on making money but making it to heaven. The prevailing religious culture of medieval Europe is obvious in the cathedrals built during this time—still the dominant architectural feature in many cities. Gregorian chant was designed to lift up the spirit and glorify God, not to agitate the lusts of the flesh. Arthurian romance began to develop in this period, centered in the quest for the Holy Grail, whose discovery is granted only to the knight who is pure in heart.

The greatest poet of this age was Dante, whose detailed exploration of heaven and hell in *The Divine Comedy* could only have been written in such a religiously-minded cultural period. Dante Alighieri was born in Florence in 1265, at the height of the Middle Ages. "Midway upon the journey of our life," he begins his great poem, "I found myself in a dark wood, where the right way was lost" (1). He describes the bewilderment felt by many middle-aged persons as he speaks in the first-person, but as he does so, he establishes himself as an allegorical figure representing all people everywhere. The "dark wood" symbolizes the world that leads men astray from the straight and narrow way. Dante tries to find his way back to the right path but finds his way blocked by three ferocious creatures: a leopard, symbolizing the temptations of the flesh; a lion, symbolizing pride; and a wolf, symbolizing avarice. Here, in medieval allegory, we encounter a completely new kind of literature, thoroughly Christian and centered in man's pilgrimage to everlasting life.

Dante encounters the poet Virgil, who is to guide him through hell. But the pagan poet, for all his virtue, explains that he cannot usher Dante into Paradise, "for that Emperor who reigns there above wills not, because I was rebellious to His law" (2). So they enter the gate upon which is written the words, "Leave every hope, ye who enter!" (4). Down into the Inferno they go, seeing all sorts of sinners—including not a few wicked popes—in eternal torment, each getting his just deserts, with everything described in lurid detail. The moral agenda here, of course, is to warn the sinner of the consequences of his misconduct.

Eventually they come to purgatory, where Virgil takes his leave and the pure Christian Beatrice guides Dante upward, higher and higher, even into the realms of Paradise. When you think about it, the dramatic strategy of Dante in this poem is truly astonishing. Homer's epic took place on earth, even though it was characterized by free discourse between men and gods. Virgil's epic did likewise, though giving Aeneas a tour through the underworld. But here in Dante we have a major poem in which *none* of the action takes place in the real world. Even the dark wood is allegorical; everything happens in a completely different and eternal realm. It is a literature that could only be possible in a predominantly Ideational age, and one that continues to edify Christian readers to this day. In fact, the fantasies of J. R. R. Tolkien and C. S. Lewis, so popular among Christians in our time, take their inspiration directly from the allegorical literature of this period.

Progress of the Gospel

It is important to note that the Gospel continued to spread and be preserved in a number of important ways during the Middle Ages. As Holy Roman Emperor, Charlemagne set about converting the Teutonic tribes of Northern Europe. Admittedly, he used the sword, but he succeeded. Even as Islam was sweeping over the Eastern Christian territories, the Christian faith was spreading rapidly in Western and Northern Europe, England, and Ireland.

The importance of the monasteries during this developmental

time cannot be underestimated. The collapse of Roman central government in the West in the fifth century took with it the infrastructure of Latin learning. Originating in the East from groups of hermits who began to organize primitive communities in the third century, monasticism took hold in the West under the spiritual leadership of Benedict of Nursia (480-543). The Rule of Benedict regulated a life of Christian worship, study, and useful labor during a chaotic period of history. Gospel-centered learning was preserved by the monastic libraries and scriptoriums. Higher education for clergy took place in the cathedral schools overseen by the bishops of the great cities. In time, new intellectual developments in the West, plus scholarly contact with Islam, led to the establishment of universities out of the cathedral schools in centers like Naples and Paris in the eleventh and twelfth centuries. In those days, theology was the most important part of the curriculum and the subject around which all knowledge was unified. By the late Middle Ages the monasteries had become corrupted by wealth. By the Modern Period the universities became corrupted by secular thought. But in the beginning and for a long time thereafter both served the Gospel.

Another gospel element is centered in the fine arts. I have mentioned the Gregorian chant, that wonderful music that sounds so strange to us today because it is designed to appeal to the spirit and not the emotions. Closely allied to this was the development of the liturgy, the beauty and majesty of which many are rediscovering today.

The liturgy springs from very ancient sources. Traditionally, the first part of the service consists of the formal reading of Scripture with exposition by a minister. This has its origins in the Jewish synagogue. "On the Sabbath day he [Jesus] went into the synagogue, as was his custom. And he stood up to read" (Luke 4:16). In His sermon on Isaiah 61:1-2 Jesus startled everyone by announcing that He was the Messiah. The second part of the historic liturgy is the celebration of Holy Communion. At the end of His earthly ministry Jesus took the ancient Jewish rite of Passover and made it His own, the Lord's

Supper. Henceforth the preaching of the Word and the administration of the Sacrament of the Altar became the two focal points of the Christian liturgy. Communion was celebrated every Sunday in the early Church, as it still is in liturgical churches. So integral were these things that St. Augustine called the Lord's Supper "the visible Word."

The elements of the liturgy express the Gospel in a simple way. Music students learn the parts of the mass with a simple acrostic: "King George Can't Speak American." The first letters of each word stand for *Kyrie, Gloria, Credo, Sanctus*, and *Agnus Dei. Kyrie* means "Lord" from the phrase, "Lord, have mercy." So the service begins with confession of sins. The minister pronounces the forgiveness of sins from Christ. Knowing that our sins are forgiven, we rejoice by singing the *Gloria*: "Glory be to God on high." Our faith is more than feelings; so we confess its content in the Creed. The *Credo* is so called from the first words of the Nicene Creed: "I believe." *Sanctus* means "holy," the first word in the praise song that comes before the Lord's Supper. After the bread and wine have been consecrated, the people sing a hymn to Christ as they come forward to receive His body and blood: *Agnus Dei*: "Lamb of God, You take away the sin of the world." Even if the sermon is terrible—and medieval preachers came to focus more and more on morality and allegorical interpretations of the Bible—the Gospel is still expressed in the form and words of the liturgy. It is one of those indestructible things that has come down to us from that Christian era like the Gothic cathedral: It still stands and testifies. And where it testifies, it brings people to faith.

Opposition to the Gospel

If the Gospel is expressed clearly in the liturgy, then the devil will attack the liturgy to get at the Gospel in it. Thus there arose the eucharistic controversy of the ninth century led by a monk named Radbertus. The historic understanding of the Church concerning the Lord's Supper was that Christ was speaking literally when He said,

"This is my body" (Matthew 26:26). That is, His body and blood are really and truly present in, with, and under the bread and wine of Holy Communion. If Christ had meant us to understand the sacrament as symbolic, He would have said, "This *represents* My body." But He did not. Therefore we are bound to His words as recorded in the Bible. The bread is bread but also the body of Christ. Likewise with the wine.

The nature of the Lord's Supper is like the nature of Christ, however. The mind of man cannot grasp the simple yet unfathomable truth that as Christ is both human and divine, the Sacrament is both bread and body. The Holy Gospel is at stake here, for if the bread is the body, then Christ is present; and where Christ is present, there is forgiveness of sins, life, and salvation. This the devil cannot abide. Nor can human thought abide such apposite mysteries and so tends to engage in extreme interpretations, either adding to Scripture or taking away. Concerning the nature of Christ, Arius took something away in emphasizing His human nature over the divine. Concerning the nature of the Sacrament, Radbertus added something by emphasizing the body over the bread. He claimed that the bread was *changed into* the body of Christ, a doctrine that came to be known as *transubstantiation*. Controversy raged, and able theologians such as Ratramnus defended the traditional, orthodox understanding of the Sacrament. But gradually the views of Radbertus gained acceptance, and the false doctrine was ratified by the Fourth Lateran Council in 1215, reaffirmed by the Council of Trent in 1551, and continues to be taught in Rome today. Needless to say, this error opposes the Gospel; in fact, it borders on idolatry. Crowds would worship the consecrated host in the *Corpus Christi* processions. Superstitious people came to steal pieces of consecrated bread and take them home as talismans. Hence the development of individual communion wafers so widely used today. And the controversy concerning the Lord's Supper, once begun, has never been resolved.

We have concentrated thus far on the Western church. Meanwhile the Eastern church, centered in the imperial city of Constantinople, was challenged by the rising power of Islam. It is fair to say that after the Seven Ecumenical Councils of the early Church (325-870) there *was* no theological development in the East. The doctrine and worship continued pretty much as they had been since the fifth century, and remain so to this day. In the church of Rome, the word of the pope became the *de facto* final authority in matters of faith and life. In the Eastern church, with no pope, tradition came to assume the same role. In both churches, Scripture is held as divinely inspired, inerrant, and infallible; but it is not the sole source of doctrine. Scripture is one factor, and in the Eastern church it is part of the tradition handed down by the fathers.

Along with this adherence to tradition in the Eastern church came a concomitant problem: Error came to be as firmly entrenched as truth. Nestorius (d. 451), for example, rose to become patriarch of Constantinople. He taught that Christ became the Son of God by adoption, not by virtue of His having been begotten by His Father before all worlds. Having been adopted, Christ is "monophysite"; that is, He has only one nature. In eternity He no longer remains human but is divine only. The threat to the Gospel here is that Christ is made less than He actually is. The complete revelation of Scripture about Him is diminished.

This Monophysite heresy was condemned but continued to spread. Not only did it make the Eastern church vulnerable to Islam—which also held a lower view of Christ—but it strained relations with the Western church. To counteract this error, Western theologians added the term *filioque* ("and the Son") to the Latin translation of the Nicene Creed. Henceforth the Third Article read, "And I believe in the Holy Spirit, the Lord and giver of life, who proceeds from the Father *and the Son. . . .*" The reason for this was to emphasize the true and complete divinity of Christ after His resurrection and ascension as well as the dual procession of the Holy Spirit. This is clearly shown in the Gospel of John, where Jesus says on one hand, "the Holy Spirit, whom *the Father will send* in my name," and on the other, "when the

Counselor comes, whom *I will send* to you from the Father" (14:26; 15:26). In the ensuing *filioque* controversy, the doctrine of the dual procession was rejected by the East. This led to the first major schism in Christianity, the split between the Eastern and Western churches in 1054. Pope and patriarch excommunicated each other.

Continuity of the Gospel

Even so, the Gospel was never absent from the Church during the Middle Ages. How could it be? Christ promised to build His church with Himself, or to put it another way, the doctrine of justification by faith as the chief cornerstone. If the Gospel was retained in the liturgy and in the Lord's Supper, it was also expressed most beautifully in the cathedrals built during these centuries. Most of them are cruciform; that is, the basic floor plan is designed to show a great cross, reminding the worshiper of the source of his hope of redemption. The details also communicate the Gospel, with Bible stories illustrated in stone carvings and stained glass. These edifices have truly been called "sermons in stone." From time to time gifted preachers such as Bernard of Clairvaux (1090-1153) would arise to proclaim the Gospel in those magnificent houses of worship. St. Bernard was particularly esteemed by Luther for his love of the Bible and his teaching of justification by faith. In addition, the Gospel found expression in a tangible fashion through the medieval mystery plays from which the modern theater traces its origins. One of the most poignant of these shows Abraham and Isaac ascending Mt. Moriah (the chancel steps), with the child asking the father where the sacrifice is going to come from. Also pageants, such as the Towneley Cycle from England, depicted all of the major stories of the Bible. Often these pageants were shown on horse-drawn carts (like floats) drawn through the streets of the city, while others were presented in stations out-of-doors, with the crowds walking from one scene to another.

We have seen how the poetry of a given period has been an accurate indicator of its cultural mode. A hymn is properly the text, not the tune. The text is poetry. Poetry is literature. With this in mind we see that the literature of the Church—expressed in hymns—continued to witness to the Gospel throughout the Medieval Period. Many of these are still in use today, as a glance at the hymnal will show.

From the time when Latin was a living language comes Fortunatus (530-609), who wrote:

> *The royal banners forward go;*
> *The cross shows forth redemption's flow*
> *Where he, by whom our flesh was made,*
> *Our ransom in his flesh was made.*
>   *Lutheran Worship (LW), 103*

Note the tone of this hymn. It is an objective statement of faith, without a single first person personal pronoun (I, me, my, myself). Yet at the same time it praises God who has made this salvation possible for us through Jesus Christ. Here we see that theology is doxology.

Similar is the work of Theodulf of Orleans (760-821), who also wrote in Latin. Many know his lines, inspired by the triumphal entry of Christ into Jerusalem just before his Passion:

> *All glory, laud, and honor*
> *To you, Redeemer, King,*
> *To whom the lips of children*
> *Made sweet hosannas ring.*
> *You are the king of Israel*
> *And David's royal Son,*
> *Now in the Lord's name coming,*
> *Our king and Blessed One.*
>   LW, 102

The common people had always retained the right of congregational singing in their own tongue. From the German hymnody of around the year 1100 comes a great Easter hymn:

> *Christ is arisen*
> *From the grave's dark prison.*
> *So let our song exulting rise:*
> *Christ with comfort lights our eyes.*
> *Alleluia!*
>
> LW, 124

One of my personal favorites is a twelfth-century hymn by Bernard of Cluny, a hymn that sings of the church triumphant, finally secure with Christ in eternity, filled with everlasting joy and peace:

> *Jerusalem the golden,*
> *With milk and honey blest,*
> *Beneath your contemplation*
> *Sink heart and voice oppressed.*
> *I know not, oh, I know not*
> *What joys await us there,*
> *What radiancy of glory,*
> *What bliss beyond compare.*
>
> LW, 309

Many more could be adduced to strengthen the argument that the Gospel continued to be proclaimed in the hymns of the Western church throughout the Middle Ages.

Erosion of Ideational Culture

I have argued that every dominant cultural mode, Sensate or Ideational, somehow contains within itself the seeds of its own destruction. The Sensate Roman culture just kept hurtling onward in the direction that had sustained it in the past. One military conquest succeeded another until there was far too much empire to administer efficiently. Sensual indulgence turned into wanton depravity. So too with the Ideational Middle Ages. What began as legitimately spiritual became superspiritual. Straightforward Romanesque architecture developed into overblown Gothic. The Sacrament of the Altar came to be seen as more spiritual than defined in the Bible. Men and women were not encouraged to live out the Christian life in their ordinary secular vocations, but to withdraw to monasteries and pursue an entirely religious life.

With this in mind we cannot leave this period without saying a word about its most eminent theologian, Thomas Aquinas (1224-1274), and the theological developments that are centered in him. Thomas is famous for his *Summa Theologica*, a compendium of dogmatics, or systematic theology, in which he combines Christian doctrine with the philosophy of Aristotle. Just why there should have been an attempt to harmonize theology and philosophy is a question that arises out of an earlier historical context.

The Church Fathers, such as Athanasius and Augustine, countered heresy with arguments taken directly from Scripture. They had been well-trained in rhetoric and the philosophical schools of their day, but their final appeal was always to God's inspired, infallible, and inerrant Word. With the beginning of the universities around 1050 and the establishment of schools of theology began the attempt to justify faith with reason. This was a time when medieval theologians loved to argue over abstruse theoretical questions. In other words, a philosophical approach allows theology to consider questions that Scripture does not answer. Or even ask.

Traditionally, Christian doctrine had been a body of precepts handed down from one generation to the next. As Jesus said, "I do nothing on my own but speak just what the Father has taught me" (John 8:28). And Paul stated, "What I received I passed on to you as of first importance: that Christ died for our sins according to the Scriptures" (1 Corinthians 15:3). Each generation had to take that received body of teaching and search the Scriptures to defend the faith against the latest heresy.

But now, with the establishment of the Church in the West and the development of medieval scholasticism, theology itself began to wander farther and farther afield from the central tenets of the Gospel.

Two schools of thought developed during this time: Nominalism and Realism. Nominalism held that only individuals and no abstract entities exist. For example, there is no abstract universal CHAIR on some ethereal plane from which all individual chairs derive. The danger inherent in this approach is that when applied to Christology it can lead to tritheism or unitarianism. Realism, on the other hand, is the doctrine that universals exist as a reality outside the mind, that an abstract term names an independent and unitary reality. This school believed in the CHAIR. The potential problem with realism is that it can lead to a schism between the spiritual and material worlds—just the sort of trap the Gnostics had fallen into a thousand years before.

Reconciling the ways of God with philosophy as Thomas attempted to do was from the start a risky enterprise, as are the current attempts to combine theology with essentially secular disciplines such as science or business. The end result is always the same: The simple biblical truth of the Gospel becomes obscured by more exciting preoccupations. And when biblical truth is mixed with anything else, there is only one result: more law. This is what began to happen to the Western church in the late Middle Ages: There came to be an increased emphasis on salvation by works. As one might expect, this legalistic atmosphere produced hypocrisy.

Monasteries became cesspools of moral depravity. Clergy—from the local priest to the curia in Rome—lived for their bellies. Bishops commanded armies, and the pope became a secular tyrant. Of course the people were not fooled. Geoffrey Chaucer (d. 1400) was a layman, and when he wrote *The Canterbury Tales* in the late fourteenth century he populated it with less-than-saintly priests and nuns. By contrast, Chaucer's Parson stands as a moral plumb line within the *Tales*, showing how a truly godly cleric should live and conduct his ministry. In this sense, Chaucer allies himself with the voices of reform that were rising in the late Middle Ages.

John Wyclif (or Wycliffe) (1320-1384), a parish priest and teacher at Oxford University, opposed the hegemony of the pope. He translated the Bible from the Latin Vulgate into English and issued a complete edition of it. This remarkable man attacked the false doctrine of transubstantiation along with the enforced celibacy of clergy—something that had been mandatory only since the twelfth century. Moreover, Wyclif taught the truth that Christ alone is the mediator between God and man and the true head of the Church. The pope, with his pretensions to supremacy over church and state, was Antichrist. No wonder they posthumously excommunicated Wyclif and desecrated his remains.

Jan Hus (1370-1415) had to face the fire in person. The Bohemian reformer was a priest and teacher at the University of Prague. He supported Wyclif's reforms and went on to attack indulgences and corruption in the church. Excommunicated in 1412, Hus turned to writing and insisted that all church dogmas and decrees must be in accord with Holy Scripture. One of his hymns is still sung today:

> *Jesus Christ, our blessed Savior,*
> *Turned away God's wrath forever;*
> *By his bitter grief and woe*
> *He saved us from the evil foe.*
> LW, 236

Here again, as in so many medieval hymns, we have an objective statement of the Gospel, full of theological depth and insight. It should be noted that the objective, theological nature of ancient and medieval hymns stems from the same impetus as the creeds: as a defense against heresy. In the worship wars of the second century the Gnostics popularized and spread their heretical ideas through popular and singable hymns. Christian hymn writers responded with orthodox songs.

Hus was summoned to appear before the Council of Constance and was promised safe conduct by the emperor. But his enemies prevailed and had him thrown into prison, from whence he was condemned and burned at the stake. Like Wyclif, his ashes were cast into the river. But the ideas of both continued to flow onward.

7

The Modern Period

There had been two previous Transitional periods in Western civilization. The first, from the seventh to the fifth centuries B.C., marked the decline of Ideational Greek culture and the rise of the Sensate Roman culture. The second, from the fourth to the sixth centuries A.D., had seen the fall of Rome and the arrival and establishment of a more Ideational Christian civilization. Now, in the sixteenth century, with a long-established Ideational mode beginning to crumble, the time was ripe for new ideas. Aquinas's attempt to unite theology and philosophy in the Middle Ages had ended with a division between the two disciplines. In time science would go its independent way. Ultimately both philosophy and science would turn and attack the Church.

As a symbolic event for the beginning of this Transition and the end of the Ideational Middle Ages, we should consider the voyage of Columbus (1492). It was partly motivated by religious concerns—Columbus wanted to convert the natives. It was partly motivated by secular concerns—Columbus was out to find a shorter trade route to India (see Figure 2, p. 48).

If the Middle Ages had been Ideational/spiritual in terms of dominant cultural values, the Modern Period by contrast came to be characterized by a more Sensate/material set of dominant cultural values.

The Transitional phase between the Middle Ages and the Modern Period falls in those centuries we have come to call the Reformation or the Renaissance, depending on which set of cultural dynamics are under consideration.

The term *renaissance* means "rebirth." What was reborn between the fourteenth and seventeenth centuries was a humanistic revival of classical learning, recovered from ancient Greece and Rome. Humanism tends to be a Sensate philosophy centered in man, not God. To be sure, there was a Christian humanism exemplified by such scholars as Erasmus, More, and Melanchthon. They brought the worthwhile elements of the classical revival to bear on Christian studies. Erasmus, for example, produced the first critical edition of the Greek New Testament. This *Textus Receptus* became the basis for the New Testament of the King James Version of the Bible (1611). But a secular humanism soon developed apart from the Church, and this became the cornerstone of the modern outlook. To the dismay of churchmen in the West, this was to be the wave of the future.

Yet just at this Transitional period we have another kind of rebirth taking place, a spiritual renewal we have come to call the Reformation. Part of its impetus is medieval, with a love of the Western church and a heartfelt desire to purify it of its abuses; part of it is modern, with its emphasis on the conscience of the individual believer. Yet another part of it is ancient, drawing theological inspiration from St. Paul and St. Augustine. All of it is an anomaly in a rising secular era, and an indication that no matter what particular phase of Western civilization may be going on, the words of Jesus Christ will always prevail. He will build His Church. The Gospel will be proclaimed in all the world.

It is interesting to note that the Christian faith—a paradoxical balance of Ideational and Sensate elements—seems to have had some of its most notable successes during times of cultural transition. As the Sensate Roman Empire crumbled, Christianity spread far and wide. And the Reformation period saw the restoration of Bible-based doctrine and practice.

The Reformation

What was at stake in the Reformation? The same thing as in all church fights throughout all ages: the Gospel. The birth date of the Reformation is generally acknowledged to be October 31, 1517, the day Martin Luther (1485-1546) nailed the Ninety-five Theses to the church door at Wittenberg. This document is ostensibly a manifesto against indulgences, those certificates issued by the pope that granted forgiveness not only for sins you had committed, but even for sins you were *planning* to commit. And if you could afford it, you could buy forgiveness for the sins of others. The theology of indulgences was based firmly on the doctrine of works-righteousness—a doctrine that, as we have seen, was a heretical (from Pelagius) departure from the best theological tradition of the Western church. Holy people such as monks and saints did so many good deeds that not only were they able to earn their own salvation, they had built up a kind of savings account comprised of works of *supererogation*. The church of Rome claimed authority to sell this excess merit.

Johann Tetzel (1465-1519), a Dominican friar and indulgence salesman par excellence, would cry, "As soon as the coin in the coffer rings, a soul from purgatory springs." The common people were being fleeced, and their money flowed into Rome to build St. Peter's Basilica. Against this abuse, Thesis 62 stands as the central tenet of the entire Reformation: "The true treasure of the church is the most holy gospel of the glory and grace of God." That is, papal decrees that are not in full agreement with the Word of God are worthless. The only thing that matters, and the central task of the Church, is the proclamation of justification by grace through faith as taught by Scripture. And that alone.

Luther, an accomplished musician and law student in his youth, later became an Augustinian monk and took holy orders. His aptitude for study led to his appointment as professor of Old Testament at the new University of Wittenberg. Even as his star was rising, the labyrinth of medieval theology with its convoluted philosophical method left him more and more confused. The root issue was how a man can be reconciled to a just and angry God. By prayer? By fasting? Mortification of the flesh? Confession? Try as he might, Luther could not find peace of mind in anything the Church offered.

Then, in 1514, he was preparing a lecture on Psalm 71. Again and again the psalmist sings of the righteousness of God in a positive sense: "My mouth shall show forth thy righteousness and thy salvation all the day" (Psalm 71:15, KJV). God was righteous, to be sure, but this righteousness was something to be feared, not loved. Yet the psalmist associates God's righteousness with His salvation. A perplexing passage indeed. Late at night in his study Luther wrestled with this seeming contradiction. Then he came across a verse in Galatians: "Clearly no one is justified before God by the law, because, 'The righteous will live by faith'" (Galatians 3:11). Suddenly it clicked. This is the Good News! The righteousness of God is something imputed, given to human beings as a free gift because of Christ's death and resurrection. Righteousness is something God has but gives to those who believe in Jesus. So we need not fear the righteousness of God anymore. We are not saved by works, as the pope taught, but by faith. It is said that Luther scribbled the word *sola* ("alone") in the margin of his Latin Bible next to the word for faith. Hence the Reformation motto: *sola fides.* "By faith alone."

Luther succeeded where Wyclif and Hus had failed. Why? Somehow various external factors came together just at this time. A technological revolution in communications facilitated the spread of Luther's ideas. The printing press, invented by Johannes Gutenberg in the mid-fifteenth century, made possible the transmission of Reformation thought faster than it could be stamped out by Roman church authorities. In addition, the tradition of street singing by wandering minstrels facilitated the spread of the new theology by means of Luther's hymns. Luther's first hymn, *Ein neues lied wir heben an* ("We now lift up a new song"), was really a political broadside or protest song, written after two Evangelical monks were killed for preaching the Gospel. Most famous of course is the universally-known "A Mighty Fortress Is Our God," which like medieval vernacular hymns is an objective statement of faith.

Like Wyclif, Luther believed the common people should have access to the Bible in their own language. Luther, however, in accordance with the new humanism, made his translation into German from the original Greek and Hebrew. Consistent with the tradition of the ancient creeds, the Lutherans submitted to the emperor a statement of their teachings in the Augsburg Confession of 1530. When Cardinal Cajetan, the papal legate, was asked by the emperor if he could refute this new teaching he replied, "Yes, but not with Scripture."

That the Reformers should have done this under the auspices of the state is a matter of some controversy. Recall that after the collapse of the Roman Empire in the West, government turned to the Church for protection. During the Middle Ages, when the Church was the dominant cultural influence, the state was subordinate to the Church or at least was seen as an institution comprised of Church members with values in harmony with the Christian faith. Now in the Reformation period, with the fledgling Protestant church in jeopardy, it was natural for the Church to turn to the state for protection. There had always been a close alliance between the two institutions; all magistrates were Church members. But now on the negative side it was the full intention of the church of Rome to use the military forces of the state to exterminate the Lutherans as soon as the Muslims—who were just at that time laying siege to Vienna—could be turned back. Among the signatories of the Augsburg Confession were Elector John of Saxony, one of the most powerful political figures of the day. So the state church developed in Lutheran Germany. But in a rising secular culture, what began as a harmonious cooperation was not to last.

The new proclamation of justification by faith was gaining adherents everywhere. Reformation spread rapidly throughout Western

Europe, continuing in Switzerland through the ministry of Frenchman John Calvin (1509-1564). Where Luther was an exegete, Calvin was a systematician, producing a magisterial volume of dogmatic theology in his *Institutes of the Christian Religion*. It has been said that Luther stressed the glory of God's love, and Calvin stressed the love of God's glory. That is, the central tenet in Calvin's theology was the sovereignty of God, and the obligation of humanity to comply with his will. Calvin, along with fellow reformer William Farel, succeeded in reorganizing the city of Geneva, Switzerland, along Protestant lines, establishing a functional theocracy. This reflected the "regulative principle" in which church and civil government and life were ordered strictly according to the principles of the New Testament. For example, Calvin held that only Psalms were to be allowed to be sung in worship services, whereas Luther himself was a hymn writer. The lively metrical Psalms, called "Geneva jigs," were marvels of congregational song. Calvinism took hold in England in the mid-sixteenth century beginning with King Edward VI and continuing with Queen Elizabeth. It is one of the ironies of literary history that the greatest age of English poetry produced practically no hymns. Nevertheless, Calvinism swept into England and through the Puritans became the dominant religious outlook of the emerging American colonies.

Wherever the Gospel breaks out, it is counterattacked by the devil. The stability and slow pace of medieval theological development was now a thing of the past. New religious groups, each more radical than the last, sprang up like weeds in springtime. In Germany one group taught that it was possible to receive direct, immediate revelations from God, apart from Holy Scripture. Just as the Montanists had done in the second century. In England another group held that spiritual people could not be hurt by sin, and tried to prove it by cursing and indulging in fornication. Just as the Gnostics had done in the first century. Freemasonry, the father of all modern lodges, began in the early eighteenth century. These were and are secret religious societies that offer fellowship and hospitality to members while their teachings deny the divinity of Christ. A logical extension of what the Arians had done in the fourth century.

The Roman Catholic Church was forced by the Reformation to make changes, especially by cleaning up corruption in the monasteries and electing popes of good moral character. The Society of Jesus, better known as the Jesuits, was founded in 1540 and became instrumental in the (often forced) reconversion of Protestants. Reforms were also carried forward by the Council of Trent, which met in three sessions between 1545 and 1563. Bishops were henceforth required to actually live in their dioceses, a good thing, but the Protestant—not to say biblical—doctrine of justification by faith was condemned, a very bad thing. In time the church that once sent armies against the Muslims in Palestine during the Crusades now began to send troops against its fellow Christians in Protestant lands. It is estimated that a third of the population of Germany was destroyed during the Thirty Years' War, 1618-1648. The Gospel was opposed by force of arms. It has been said that the religious wars of the sixteenth and seventeenth centuries exhausted the capacities of Europe for religious controversy, preparing the way for a more secular culture that had been rising all along.

The Renaissance: Transitional

The Renaissance, according to the *World Book Encyclopedia*, "was a great cultural movement that began in Italy during the early 1300's. It spread to England, France, Germany, the Netherlands, Spain, and other countries in the late 1400's and ended about 1600." Thus began a change in the cultural atmosphere, a rediscovery and re-appreciation of the classical civilization of Greece and Rome. From our perspective, this was a Transitional period, with a mix of Sensate and Ideational cultural values.

The currents of this new period of civilization were reflected in all of the arts, particularly poetry. Petrarch (1304-1374) invented the sonnet form during this time, touching off a centuries-long vogue of writing poetry about human love. Yet he could also write an essentially religious work, *De contemptu mundi* (*Of Contempt for the World*). So impressed was Petrarch by the advanced civilization in which he lived that he coined a term to describe the chaotic period in Europe after the fall of Rome. He called it "the Dark Ages."

In general, the Renaissance reached northern Europe and England much later. But even Geoffrey Chaucer (ca. 1343-1400), normally classified as a medieval writer, shows some influence of early Renaissance Italian writers. Petrarch and Boccaccio (1313-1375) were still living and writing at the time of Chaucer's visit to Italy on state business in 1372. While it is not known whether Chaucer actually met these poets, he certainly was influenced by their writings. His great satirical love poem, *Troilus and Criseide* (1385), is directly based on Boccaccio's *Il Filostrato*. Transitional periods are always complex, with swirling currents of influence rising and falling. In general, though, the farther you go into the Renaissance, the more secular or Sensate the culture becomes as the Ideational Middle Ages recedes into the past. Chaucer is markedly religious in his preoccupations, Shakespeare, two centuries later, less so.

William Shakespeare (1564-1616) brings character development to the foreground in his plays, while earlier playwrights wrote allegories. As my own father ages, I understand King Lear more and more. And what young man, forced too soon into grown-up conflict, does not identify with Hamlet? Then there is Falstaff, arguably Shakespeare's—and perhaps any playwright's—greatest creation. The jolly, fat, carousing, bragging corrupter of princes was killed off in *Henry V* but brought back by popular demand (like Sherlock Holmes after Reichenbach Falls) for an encore in *The Merry Wives of Windsor*. The pages of Shakespeare teem with such vivid, true-to-life creations, helping us understand why his poetry, unlike Milton's, is continually in vogue, and his plays, unlike Ben Jonson's, are continually in production. He has been well-named "the mirror of mankind."

And yet for all the Sensate realism in this great author of a

Transitional period, there is, as one might expect, a strain of Ideational thought, an element of Christian concern. Falstaff carries a "dagger of lath," that is, of wood, a clear indication that for all his vividness he is still the allegorical character Vice from the Medieval Morality Plays. Theologians of the Middle Ages had classified human frailty into the categories of the Seven Deadly Sins: pride, envy, wrath, sloth, avarice, gluttony, and lechery. Many of Shakespeare's tragedies are explorations of these vices. *Coriolanus*, for example, is the tragedy of a Roman general whose pride leads to his downfall. "Was ever man so proud as this?" ask the citizens (I.i.252). "Come not between the dragon and his wrath," warns King Lear, a man whose anger leads him into folly and madness (I.i.122). Most notably, there are in Shakespeare's plays a number of "resurrection scenes," the most famous being the overpowering climax of *The Winter's Tale* in which Queen Hermione, presumed dead throughout most of the play, is in the end presented as a statue that "miraculously" comes back to life. In general, however, these Christian aspects of Shakespeare are in the background, while the character and plot concerns are in the foreground. Chaucer is more Ideational, less Sensate; Shakespeare is more Sensate, less Ideational.

The Modern Period: Sensate

Scholars debate the beginning of the Modern Period; some place it at the French Revolution (1789), others in the twentieth century. For our purposes here I take a broader view, defining the Modern Period of Western civilization as an extended Sensate, materialistic period beginning in the sixteenth century and continuing into the twentieth. Secular preoccupations may be seen in the rise of the nation-state during this time, along with the advancement of commerce and with it commercial cities. In the medieval cities, the cathedral was the dominant architectural feature. In modern cities, business buildings determine the skyline.

If the Modern Period is secular in tone, it is also characteristically optimistic. Columbus expected to succeed in his expedition, just as Americans expected to reach the moon. Scientists knew their discoveries would improve life for many people. Politicians were certain a better world was just around the corner. Sir Thomas More wrote his *Utopia* in the sixteenth century, now called the Early Modern Period by common consent in the academic community. The generally accepted cultural values of the Modern Period are centered not in the divine but in the human, not in the spiritual but in the material. These Sensate values found expression during the Modern Period in two modes: Rationalism, which focused on human reason, and Romanticism, which concentrated on human feelings.

Rationalism

In 1662 the Royal Society was established in England to further scientific inquiry. This event was characteristic of a new element in the Modern Era: Rationalism. In general, the finest minds of this period were occupied more with reason than with revelation. As A. E. Housman says, "Man occupied himself by choice with thoughts which do not range beyond the sphere of his own understanding. Rationalism was almost deified" (Untermeyer, 503). The Christian faith experienced setbacks, not due to overt persecution as it had under the Roman Empire, but because of a certain ambient oppression stemming from a changing climate of opinion. "The most important aspect of the Restoration period is the increased challenge of various forms of secular thought to the old religious orthodoxies that had been matters of life and death since the Reformation. . . . As the 17th century drew to a close, its temper became more secular, tolerant, and moderate" (Abrams, I, 1772-1773). Symbolic of this new, now purely Sensate cultural dynamic is the rationalistic declaration of French mathematician and philosopher René Descartes: "I think, therefore I am" (see Figure 2, p. 48).

Alexander Pope was the foremost poet of this period, with his exaltation of human reason: "The powers of all subdued by thee alone, / Is not thy reason all these powers alone?" (2268). Not surprisingly, his focus is secular: "Know then thyself, presume not God to scan / The proper study of mankind is Man" (2270). And optimistic: "Spite of pride, in erring reason's spite, / One truth is clear: Whatever is, is right" (2270). It is worth remembering that America's formative years occurred during the Enlightenment or Rationalistic Period. In spite of the significant influence of Christianity, many of the dominant figures among the founding fathers, such as Benjamin Franklin and Thomas Jefferson, were rationalistic deists rather than Trinitarian Christians.

Romanticism

William Wordsworth (1770-1850) developed a Romantic poetry of feeling and sensibility. It reacted against Rationalism, but like Rationalism it centered in specifically human, or Sensate, concerns. A growing reaction to the classicism of the Enlightenment began to register in the eighteenth century with the German philosopher Emmanuel Kant (1724-1804) and his exploration of human subjectivity. Wordsworth and his friend Samuel Taylor Coleridge (1772-1834) actually traveled to Germany and attended lectures by Kant. But whether the preoccupation was upon human reason or human feelings, the cultural mode was still Sensate—centered in man and his present, material world.

The publication of *Lyrical Ballads* (1799) by Wordsworth and Coleridge marked the beginning of Romanticism in English poetry. In his famous Preface, Wordsworth defined true poetry as "the spontaneous overflow of powerful feelings"—a marked departure from the stately measure of Pope's heroic couplets (Abrams, II, 143). These feelings are often centered in nature and children. Regarding nature, Wordsworth sings, "There was a time when every meadow, grove, and stream, / The earth, and every common sight, / To me did seem / Apparelled in celestial light" (189). In Romanticism the poet begins to see nature in a new way, as something somehow immanent with the divine. Mountains are no longer big obstacles that stand in your way, but mystic temples of supernatural presence. This adulation of Nature notwithstanding, there appears in the later Wordsworth a love of London: "Earth has not any thing to show more fair / . . . This city now doth, like a garment, wear / The beauty of the morning" (Abrams, II, 198). Children, "mewling and puking" in Shakespeare's realism, are seen as vessels of the holy: "Trailing clouds of glory do we come" (190). So much for the doctrine of original sin.

American literature really began to find its voice with Romanticism and the poet Walt Whitman (1819-1892). Like Wordsworth, Whitman reveres Nature: "When I heard the learn'd astronomer, / When the proofs, the figures, were ranged in columns before me / . . . How soon unaccountable I became tired and sick, / Till rising and gliding out I wander'd off by myself, / In the mystical moist night-air, and from time to time, / Look'd up in perfect silence at the stars" (Baym, 1044-1045). The natural world is not a subject for scientific analysis, but a living entity to be revered. At the same time in the Romantics there is an optimism for and love of the city. Whitman sings of his beloved New York, "Thrive, cities—bring your freight, bring your shows, ample and sufficient rivers, / Expand" (1037).

With subjectivity comes the Romantic ego, the individual standing alone, railing against fate and defying the gods. Whitman's line, "I celebrate myself and sing myself" is lyrical but not unlike those of W. E. Henley (1849-1903): "Under the bludgeonings of chance / My head is bloody, but unbowed . . . I am the master of my fate; / I am the captain of my soul" (Baym, 1057; Abrams, II, 983).

No one would argue with the assertion that the Church has less influence on the world today than it did in the Middle Ages. We live in a secular, Sensate age. The artistic movements we have discussed have in common a general preoccupation with this world, not the world to come. The promise and the achievement of secular modern society gave the secular modern mind an optimistic outlook. But this optimism seemed to vanish in the twentieth century. Why?

Transition: Into the Postmodern

Sorokin came of age during the momentous events of the early twentieth century. Reflecting on the times in which he lived, he said: "We are living and acting at one of the epoch-making turning points of human history, when one fundamental form of culture and society—the Sensate—is declining and a different form is emerging. The indicators include increased wars, revolutions, social chaos, dictators, intellectual foment, and the destruction of human values. . . . Change of this magnitude is rare. It has happened only four times before in the thirty centuries of Western civilization" (*Crisis*, 22, 29). By this he meant previous Transitional periods of our culture, the first from Ideational Greek to Sensate Roman around the sixth century B.C., the second from Sensate Roman to Ideational Christian around the fifth century A.D., the third from Ideational Christian to Sensate Modern around the sixteenth century, and the fourth being the twentieth century in which he was living.

Sorokin's contribution was to identify this turbulent century as a Transitional period. Before it there had ensued a long Sensate period in which cultural values and presuppositions were fairly constant. The current Transitional period in which we live, he believed, would be chaotic but of limited duration. Eventually the cultural dissonance would resolve into the opposite cultural mode, and a relatively stable period of Ideational values would emerge.

Beginning of Change

This change in our culture really began to rise to the surface prior to 1900. A new note began to be heard in the poetry of the late nineteenth century, a voice of skepticism and doubt, brought on by the dizzying pace of change inherent in modern society. If the modern outlook was secular and optimistic, the new mood was secular but pessimistic. Matthew Arnold (1822-1888) advanced this query: "For what wears out the life of mortal men? / 'Tis that from change to change their being rolls; / 'Tis that repeated shocks, again, again, / Exhaust the energy of strongest souls / And numb the elastic powers" (Abrams, II, 1363).

How many everyday people felt just that way in the twentieth century? Many still do today in the twenty-first century. Arnold was not alone in having second thoughts about progress. Mark Twain (1835-1910) exhibits a real pessimism in his later work. The *fin de siecle* cynicism of Oscar Wilde (1854-1900) is well-known, though not everyone is aware that this flagrant homosexual made a deathbed confession and died a penitent Christian.

The change began to register in the other arts as well. Many Christians admire the work of the Impressionist painters, the unfocused swirls of blues and greens, not realizing the subversive subtext of this artistic movement, and how early it began to register the breakdown of modern society. The first in this line was a painting whose title lent its name to the movement, Monet's *Impression: Sunrise* (1872). Prior to Monet, painters worked with reality. You could look at a painting and say, "That's a landscape" or "That's a woman." An impression by definition deals not with what is there but with the artist's perception, or impression, of what is there. What you are looking at is not what is truly there but rather what is in the artist's mind— a radical departure from the reality-based mainstream of Western thought and art during the broader Modern Period.

From Monet, it was only a short step to the inward-focused abstract art of Kandinsky and Pollock. And what is in the artist's mind is often disturbing, to say the least. This is the complaint of the average person who visits an art gallery. She either doesn't get it or is positively offended. She is supposed to be. The purpose of the older art was to instruct and delight. The new art aims to subvert and offend. It is secular but pessimistic.

This cultural transition began to be felt also in nineteenth-century music. Functional harmony began to break down under the repeated blows of Richard Wagner (1813-1883). His astonishing *Prelude to Tristan* (1860) defies logic with its unexpected transitions from one complex chord to another, leaving one completely at a loss to find a tonal center. It perfectly expresses the rising confusion coming into a Sensate culture that is beginning to break down. It is only a short step from Wagner to the atonal music of Schoenberg or the angst-ridden cadences of Stravinsky.

These changes in literature, art, and music were indicators that the secular optimism of the broader Modern Period was breaking down and that our culture was beginning to enter a Transitional period. In looking for a historic event that symbolizes the end of the Modern Era, one must consider the sinking of the *Titanic* in 1912 (see Figure 2, p. 48). Here was the epitome of the Modern Period in all its glory, the crowning achievement of the successes of the Industrial Revolution, the biggest, the best, the fastest, the most technologically advanced, the richest, the proudest, filled with millionaires and new money, "unsink-able," and headed for the New World. The *Titanic was* the Modern Era, full steam ahead. But down she went, a harbinger of the wreck of the Modern Western civilization that was soon to follow.

Secular Pessimism

Secular pessimism really sets in with the post-World War I generation. W. B. Yeats (1865-1939) looked at the destruction of his world in the aftermath of The Great War and wrote in 1919: "Things fall apart; the center cannot hold; / Mere anarchy is loosed upon the world . . . The best lack all conviction, while the worst / Are full of passionate intensity / . . . And what rough beast, its hour come round at last, / Slouches towards Bethlehem to be born?" (Abrams, II, 1880). The poet Yeats here concurs with the negations of the scholar Spengler. More recently, Judge Robert Bork alluded to Yeats's universally-known poem in the title of his critique of Western devolution, *Slouching Toward Gomorrah*.

Contemporaneous with Yeats was the American expatriate T. S. Eliot (1888-1965). Eliot wrote his long poem *The Waste Land* during the post-World War I period and published it in 1921. Along with Schoenberg in music and Picasso in painting, Eliot stands as one of the architects of modernism in the arts. Like the other artists, he invented an entirely new form to give expression to the angst-ridden spirit of the age. So powerful was the impact of this radical new poet on English letters in the Twenties that a young Oxford student named Clive Staples Lewis, a committed secular Romantic, formed an anti-T. S. Eliot club.

The Waste Land is viewed by most critics as "a poem about spiritual dryness, about the kind of existence in which no regenerating belief gives significance and value to people's daily activities, sex brings no fruitfulness, and death heralds no resurrection" (Abrams, II, 2146). It presents to the reader a bewildering series of images with no author's voice to interpret, a fragmented form that mirrors the spiritual disintegration of people's lives in the twentieth century. In the world of the poem, religion is empty: "Son of Man / You cannot say, or guess, you know only / A heap of broken images" (2146). In contrast to modern optimism, people are now filled with a nameless dread and apprehension: "I will show you fear in a handful of dust." Where Whitman, Wordsworth, and other Romantics loved the urban areas in which they lived, Eliot depicts the "Unreal City." This is a place of death, "a rat's alley / Where the dead men lost their bones," and of empty sex, "caresses / Which are unreproved, if undesired."

The Waste Land concludes with the Hindu blessing, "Shantih shantih shantih." The Hindu religion is the ultimate negation of everything, seeing all suffering as illusion, denying the reality of reality. It is the perfect ending to the ultimate poem of despair. Ultimately

Eliot, like C. S. Lewis, could not sustain a life based upon secular principles and converted to Christianity.

These cultural earthquakes of an increasingly pessimistic secularism registered on both sides of the Atlantic. Tremors were certainly felt in the despairing novels of Ernest Hemingway and F. Scott Fitzgerald. Allen Ginsberg (1926-1997), like his fellow writer Jack Kerouac, went to Columbia University, but he did not play football there as Kerouac had done. To the contrary, he cultivated madness. His long poem *Howl* (1956) is generally acknowledged as having marked the inception of the Beat Generation. Ginsberg writes in the looping long lines originated by Whitman but is anything but optimistic in content and worldview. He is a pessimist who sees a world gone mad: "I saw the best minds of my generation destroyed by madness, starving hysterical naked" (Baym, 2698). He envisions an unreal city of lost and haunted people "who wandered around and around at midnight in the railroad yard wondering where to go, and went" (2699). The old Romantic "spontaneous overflow of powerful feelings" has in Ginsberg degenerated to furtive, perverted, illicit sex "in the grass of public parks and cemeteries" (2700). Ginsberg reserves his final imprecations for American business: "Moloch whose factories dream and croak in the fog!" (2703). In other words, he associates Capitalism with the ancient and detestable Canaanite god whom men worshiped by sacrificing their children, a vision graphically depicted thirty years earlier by Fritz Lang in *Metropolis*. Ginsberg, like Yeats and Eliot, reflects features of twentieth-century poetry that are indicative of the general state of the arts and the state of the culture. In contrast to the preceding dominant cultural mode, it is secular but pessimistic and decadent.

The term *Postmodern*, or *Pomo* for short, technically refers to a school of literary criticism that originated in France with Jacques Derrida and other scholars and became popular in American university English departments in the 1970s, especially under the influence of Stanley Fish and others at Yale. As Gene Edward Veith has shown so well in *Postmodern Times*, this philosophy is pervasive today and has a determining influence on many areas of life. It is nihilistic, destroying man's capacity to understand anything with its insistence that there is no ultimate reality and that words only refer to other words in a kind of endless series of disappearing mirrors.

Because the term *Postmodern* is linked to an academic school of thought and has gone from there to be applied generally to cultural influences that entered American society after the 1960s, I cannot use it to describe the entire twentieth century. I do contend, however, that what we call Postmodernism today is on a continuum with cultural developments that began in the late nineteenth century and continued to accelerate all through the twentieth.

It will be seen by now that we have been encountering a different system of cultural dynamics than we had perhaps supposed. Yet the view persists that Western civilization today is like that of ancient Rome. Uwe Siemon-Netto, UPI Religion Correspondent, notes that "there are serious biblical scholars today who will tell you that our era uncannily resembles the first century A.D." He cites recent work by Elian Cuvillier and Alvin J. Schmidt and points out that both societies had a unified culture, religious syncretism, and moral depravity. While those things are true to a certain extent, there are significant differences. One: First-century Rome was at the height of a Sensate cultural mode, whereas our culture is at the end of a Transitional period. Two: First-century Rome had no influence from Christianity, whereas every aspect of our civilization has been influenced by the church—as Alvin J. Schmidt correctly observes. Even during the height of the Sensate modern era, the church continued as a powerful force with the Whitefield/Wesley revivals of the eighteenth century and the great foreign missions of the nineteenth century.

Even during the chaos of the twentieth century Christianity continued to surge with the *Lutheran Hour* radio broadcasts of the twenties to the forties and the Billy Graham crusades of the fifties on. Slavery has been abolished, women have rights, education is universal, the poor are helped, the sick are cared for, and liberty continues to spread. And once the church of Jesus Christ enters a civilization, it changes everything around it and will continue to do so—no matter how small or distressed it may be—as it moves history toward its final goal.

People sense intuitively that we are living in a time of rapid change. We don't need Sorokin to tell us this. But Sorokin is helpful in pointing out that periods of rapid cultural change cannot sustain themselves for very long. You can sprint for a short distance, but if you want to cover the ground, you have to walk. In the past the long Sensate cultural mode that generally characterized Roman civilization broke down, went through a shorter, turbulent Transitional period, and resolved into the long Ideational epoch we call the Middle Ages. Then that relatively stable epoch went through a shorter, more turbulent period before resolving into the Modern Era, which began in about the sixteenth century and carried into the twentieth before breaking down decisively. At the beginning of the twentieth century only the poets could perceive it, but at the end of the century everybody could.

What we are seeing today seems to indicate that the Transitional period we are going through may be about to resolve into a new Ideational system. A century ago, secular intellectuals with a modernist worldview saw religion in decline and assumed that the trend would continue. Instead, the trend reversed. People are attracted to religion today more than ever, though not necessarily Christianity. But at present, only the poets seem to perceive it.

8

The Therian Age

There seems to be a general revival of interest in religion—or at least spirituality—underway in our culture, with corresponding indications in the fine arts. West coast artist William F. Catling says that when he first attended art school at San Francisco State in the Seventies, anyone working with religious topics was frowned upon. When he went back for his Master's in the Eighties, the atmosphere had completely changed—everyone was fascinated by "spirituality." By the Nineties, galleries all over the West Coast were featuring religious art, much of it inspired by New Age and Native American ideas but including Christian material.

Catling is a Christian artist and follows these cultural changes with considerable interest. Karen L. Mulder, founder of Christians in the Arts Networking (C.A.N.), discovered not only that there were many individual Christian artists plying their trade, but many grassroots associations of Christian artists as well. One of the most important of these is the Arts Centre Group (A.C.G.) of London, England. It was started in the Sixties by Nigel Goodwin, an actor (having studied at the Royal Academy of Dramatic Arts) and a Christian (having studied at L'Abri with Francis Schaeffer). The A.C.G. has several hundred members who meet according to their artistic discipline—poets, architects, dancers, actors, etc.—and then come together for an annual Christian arts festival.

As encouraging as these signs are, the overall tendency in the arts world seems to be against the cross. I myself established a Christian arts group in Tucson, Arizona, in the Eighties. For one of our activities we mounted a show of Catling oil paintings in the downtown arts district and brought the artist in to be present. Tucson, of course, had long been a vortex of New Age activity; the local galleries were featuring paintings and sculptures with a lot of spirituality but no Jesus. Our little show turned out to be somewhat of a guerrilla raid. I well recall the resulting intense, late-night conversations with area artists and Mr. Catling about the Christian content of his paintings.

Contemporary Poetry

Poetry likewise has reflected this trend. What scholar Norman Ault said about seventeenth-century collections of lyric poetry is, I believe, true for all. They are "the key to a historical study of poetic appreciation in the period: for together these collections reflect the taste of the century as nothing else could do" (vii). Most twentieth-century anthologies of English and American poetry contain the angst-ridden verse we have been discussing. But there is a new spiritual tone in contemporary poetry, as seen in the latest anthologies.

Some poets sing of a kind of wistful longing for religious hope. "I have a friend who still believes in heaven," writes Louise Glück in "Celestial Music." "Not a stupid person, yet with all she knows, she literally talks to god, / she thinks someone listens in heaven. / On earth, she's unusually competent. / Brave, too, able to face unpleasantness" (Bloom, 116). Glück admires her friend's religious faith. It is something she herself lacks. For whatever reason, the poet is unable to believe, and as a result she has an emptier and more difficult life. The poet has no one in heaven to listen to her problems. And on earth, the poet must confess, she is by contrast incompetent, cowardly, and weak. She identifies strongly with her friend who "still believes"; that is, she has retained something valuable that the poet once had but has lost, can't seem to find again, and regrets losing very much indeed.

This longing is captured poignantly by Mark Strand as he looks at "the book where a poet stares at the sky / And says to a blank page, 'Where, where in Heaven am I?'" (264). He is of course reversing a coarse grown-up expression to achieve poetic effect; this is the plaintive cry of a lone, lost child. He is abandoned by his eternal Father and can find no guidance from the traditional sources that maritime and spiritual navigators have always relied on—the constellations and the writings of the poets. He draws these two seemingly disparate things into parallel and makes us see how similar they really are. But in his wanderings he has no guidance. The sky is empty of stars; the page of the book of poetry is blank. Alas, he sighs, if only they were not.

When the poets express fear of an imminent apocalypse, they are betraying their Christian foundations, or at least that of the general culture. Eastern mysticism has no such climactic view of history; the world just goes on and on, and people go through endless reincarnations, hopefully evolving upward. That's not so very different from Darwinism. The Christian religion, by contrast, sees history in linear, not cyclic, terms and posits a *telos* or climactic event at the end, a final struggle between good and evil that culminates in the Second Coming of Christ. At the turn of the millennium many in American society were filled with apocalyptic expectations, much of it centered around an expected general computer crash caused by the Y2K bug. As usual with doomsday predictions, nothing happened. After all, didn't Jesus say the end would come when least expected? But the pervasive strata of Christian thought in the West makes people think this way.

Poets are sensitive to these whisperings of the collective unconscious. Jonathan Aaron draws a parallel between the Middle Ages and today in "Dance Mania": "In 1027, not far from Bernburg, / eighteen peasants were seized / by a common delusion. Holding hands, they circled for hours / in a churchyard, haunted by visions . . . And the dance mania / found its own way through time to survive / among us, as untouched as ever by the wisdom of science / . . . how many millions of us now, the living / and the dead, hand in hand as always, / approaching the brink of the millennium" (29-31). For the poet, once-mighty rational science is impotent in the face of a religious fanaticism that has persisted through the centuries and now has returned in full force. It is a macabre vision of a graveyard *Totentanz* ("dance of death" or "dance of the dead") on the edge of time, with all about to tumble into the void of universal destruction.

Donald Hall, the old pro among contemporary poets, takes a humorous approach to the end of the world in "Prophecy." Here he creates the persona of a rather cranky old Deity who thunders against the materialism of his heedless creations: "I will strike down wooden houses; I will burn aluminum / clapboard skin / I will strike down garages . . . Your children will wander looting the shopping malls / for forty years" (133-134). One must smile in acknowledgment, especially if one has teens in the house wanting to go "malling" all the time. But most poets contemplate the end of all things in a brown study, as does Brigit Pegeen Kelly in "The White Pilgrim." "A man left his home in Ohio and came East," she writes, "Dreaming he could be the dreamed-of Rider / in St. John's Revelations [sic] . . . The White Rider may come . . . but who will be left standing" (160, 162). Kelly draws on biblical imagery to rebuke society, rather like the poets-*vates* ("poet-prophets") of the old school who saw their office in terms of moral instruction. When the poet asks who will be left standing, the reader asks in response, "Will I?"

For all this, our poets reflect a generally negative view of Christianity. Amy Clampitt in "My Cousin Muriel" refers to "the evangel-haunted prairie hinterland" (84). Clampitt describes the prairie with the pejorative term "hinterland," something like a waste-land, devoid of civilization. More serious is the idea of an area—mean-ing the people of the area—being "evangel-haunted." It is an image of wild-eyed fanatics driven by implacable demons to destructive and violent acts. Like opposing abortion, I suppose. Flannery O'Connor uses the term "Christ-haunted" to describe her fellow Christians, but I doubt that Clampitt is quite as sympathetic to the Faith. O'Connor was Catholic and Southern and treated her region and religion with both sympathy and realism. The context of this poem casts aspersions on both the geography and the belief.

Carolyn Creedon has developed a theology of the absence of God in "litany." "The idea of a god here is meant to be mercurial," she explains, "a god that can leave you, disappear" (309). The poem is skillfully and poignantly written as a dialogue between two lovers. Finally the lover asks, "How will I know how you love me?" To which the voice that represents the Deity clearly states, "i have left you. that is how you will know" (90). Note how God speaks in the first person but with a lower-case i. It lowers the great I AM to our level, like the Greek myths with their passions, fights, and intrigues. Furthermore, it elevates the lover to existential solo flight status. She doesn't need her god any more than a fish needs a bicycle. He is doing her a favor by leaving. She is now liberated, able to stand on her own, bravely alone in the universe. She can get along just fine without him, thank you very much.

Thomas M. Disch takes a more aggressive stance. His closet drama, "The Cardinal Detoxes," was actually produced in New York over the protests of the Roman Catholic Church. Bitter and vindictive against his native church as only Catholics seem to be, Disch creates an alcoholic Cardinal who causes a car wreck in which a woman is killed. "God," he muses, "For the most part I do without / Him. Don't we all. He leaves us no choice, / Having left us" (91). Here again is the absence of God, but there is nothing benign about it as in Creedon. It is destructive, with religious power vested in the hands of dangerous men who destroy the lives of innocent people.

As Christianity is held in contempt by the poets, Eastern religion is seen in a more positive light. A. R. Ammons, in his Pulitzer Prize-winning long poem *Garbage*, uses traditional Western religious terms such as "eternity," "heaven," "hallelujah," and "sanctification." The dump is a metaphor of the world, and in it the garbageman is poet and priest. For all this, the basic outlook of the poem is Hindu: "all is one, one all" (49). Recycling in the poem stands for the Hindu doctrine of reincarnation, a world in which "the spirit was forever / and is forever, the residual and informing / energy" (52). Charles Wright, another Pulitzer Prize winner, explicitly draws on Buddhism in "*Disjecta Membra*" (Latin for "scattered parts"): "Zen says, stand by the side of your thoughts / As you might stand by the bank of a wide river . . . God is a scattered part, / syllable after syllable, his name asunder. / No first heaven, no second / . . . Take a loose rein and a deep seat . . . I'm emptied, ready to go . . . do what the clouds do" (288, 292, 296-297). The old Christian God, an anthropomorphized heavenly Father, is reduced to shards and fragments, a "scattered part." Those who are awake like the Buddha will let go of all desire and simply drift along like a river or like the clouds.

What are our poets telling us about ourselves and about our society? There is a religious impulse in us, a certain spark that responds to religious teaching. The dry grit of secular humanism and empirical scientific knowledge cannot sustain us. We need a Deity. But the God of the Bible, with His paradoxes and call to sacrificial living, His bloody redemption plan with the claims of Jesus to be the Son of God who rose from the dead—there we draw the line. We want something a little more reasonable, but at the same time something different, something we can come and go from, like dinner at a Chinese restaurant. Many Chinese restaurants these days feature buffets, allowing the customer not only to come and go but to pick and choose. Instead of one big plate of chop suey, you can have a little of this and a little of that. Not all of it sits harmoniously in the stomach. Something like this seems to be going on in our culture theologically as well as gastronomically. People try to nourish their souls with the most indigestible bits of incompatible beliefs.

The New Age, Etc.

One of the most difficult aspects of cultural analysis is trying to get a grip on the strange concatenation of influences known collectively as the New Age movement. In reality, as we will see, an Ideational shift in the entire culture is much more far-reaching than the kind of New Age mysticism you find at the local crystal shop. Like the hobo's mulligan stew, it's got a little bit of everything thrown into one pot, and as it boils away you see now one thing, now another appear on the surface, then slide into the depths. One glimpse shows an influence of traditional Zen Buddhism. Another reveals a trace of ancient mythology. Here is a whiff of pagan Wicca, mixed in with deep environmentalism. Over there medical doctors schooled in the scientific method are experimenting with yoga meditation techniques. For all this confusion of sources, it may be helpful to factor out some of the streams of thought that empty into this swirling cauldron of spirituality. People call it the New Age movement, but it is much broader in scope. Much of it originates in the Far East, especially India and China.

Hinduism

Hinduism is so old no one can trace the source. Unlike Christianity, it can identify no single charismatic founder and has no single holy book as the source of its doctrines. Hinduism is polytheistic; in its pantheon are many gods. Millions, in fact. However, taken together these gods comprise and are manifestations of one world-spirit, which they call Brahman. Three of the most important are Brahma (the creator), Vishnu (the preserver), and Shiva (the destroyer). As with many heathen religions, a chief female deity is very important. In Hinduism, this is the wife of Shiva, called by various names, including Uma, the revered goddess of motherhood, and Kali, the terrifying goddess of destruction. Movie buffs will recall that in the movie *Gunga Din*, Cary

Grant and his companions fought against the Thugs, members of a murderous cult that worshipped Kali.

There are four main collections of writings in Hinduism, and they include theology, philosophy, epics, and myths. Best known of the six schools of Hindu philosophy is *yoga,* a system of mental and physical exercises designed to free the soul from dependence on the body and this material world and to unite the soul with Brahman, the universal spirit. The metaphor of a drop of water merging with the ocean is often used to describe this spiritual journey. Obviously, there is no notion here of a person retaining an eternal identity as an individual. Related to this are the concepts of reincarnation and *karma.* According to the law of karma, everything you do, whether good or bad, has an impact on your life now and on your next life. If things are going badly for you, it may be because you had done something evil in a previous life. When you die, your soul is immediately reborn or reincarnated, but either higher or lower on the phylogenetic scale, according to your good or bad karma. Hopefully you will move up and out in a kind of spiritual evolution, until finally in your last reincarnation you escape from this cycle and your soul is merged with the All. To help you attain this *moksha,* or new level of existence, there are spiritual guides called gurus. Fortunately there is plenty of time for all this striving, since not only the individual soul goes through cycles, but also the world itself as Uma/Kali generates and destroys. So the wheel turns.

These views have filtered into the West. In academic circles, a form of this cyclic view of history is seen in Toynbee. In popular music, a song called "Take Your Place on the Great Mandala" was recorded by Peter, Paul, and Mary in the Sixties. Later on, in the Eighties, country singer Willie Nelson came out with "It's Just a Little Old-fashioned Karma Comin' Down." Hindu ideas filter down to the man on the street.

Perhaps more noteworthy, though, is the fact that Hinduism produces no congregations as we in the West understand them. There are community festivals, of course, but worship on an ongoing basis is essentially an individual enterprise. You pick your god, buy an idol, set up a shrine in your home or garden, and there offer your prayers, incense, and offerings. Hindu temples are full of images of the gods, with individuals coming and going in religious observance. One can see the appeal for individualistically-minded Americans who say when confronted with the demands of creedal Christianity, "I have my own beliefs." You get your crystal and your incense and some books you like and set up a shrine in your home or garden. New Age religion facilitates a designer *cultus,* or system of religious practice. Note the fundamental contrast between East and West: Christianity is communal in this life, individual in the next; Hinduism is individual in this life, communal in the next. That is to say, we Christians gather in communities for worship, and in our doctrinal confessions we all say the same thing; yet we believe that just as Christ is risen from the dead and retains His identity in eternity, so we will be ourselves, body and soul, forever and ever. Hinduism, by contrast, is personal and individualistic in the outworking and application of religion in the present, but the ultimate goal is the negation of self.

Buddhism

Buddhism derives from Hinduism. About 500 B.C. Siddhartha Gautama was born in India to wealth and privilege. Perturbed by the suffering of mankind, he left his wife and small child to become a spiritual seeker. It is not recorded how his family may have suffered on account of his seeking. After years of wandering, he became enlightened. When asked by his disciples who he was, he replied, "I am awake." His insight was that the Hindu cycle of birth and death, pain and suffering was caused by attachment to material things. One must break out of this cycle through meditation and strive to attain a state of nonattachment and perfect peace called nirvana. Just like the rock group, but without drugs. Where Hinduism was largely confined to

India, Buddhism spread rapidly throughout Asia, making great progress in China and Tibet. Zen Buddhism originated in China but took hold in Japan, with its emphasis on achieving *satori* (enlightenment) through a sudden flash of insight. Zen masters would train their disciples by use of the *koan*, a contradictory question whose pondering would lead to *satori*. In the West, the best known of these is, "What is the sound of one hand clapping?" Answer: "The sound of silence." Baby Boomers will remember that this was the title of a million-selling folk-rock song by Simon and Garfunkel in the early Sixties.

Taoism

Taoism is more difficult to pin down, having had no definite historical origins as did Buddhism. There is a superstitious Chinese folk religion known by the same name, but Taoism as a system of philosophical spirituality is something entirely different. The term *tao* (pronounced "doe") means "the way." Its legendary founder, Lao Tsu, was supposedly born at age seventy around 300 B.C. He left a book called the *Tao Te Ching*, a collection of sayings including one that is now well-known in the West: "The journey of a thousand miles begins with but a single step." Confucianism emphasized duty, ceremony, public service, and a well-ordered society. The Tao, by contrast, stressed living a simple and spontaneous life close to nature, engaging in contemplation and meditation, and avoiding conventional social obligations. You can see why this was appealing to Sixties hippies. It was also appealing to certain influential Catholics. Thomas Merton, the noted Catholic author and Trappist monk, wrote a book on the subject: *The Way of Chuang Tzu*. When was it published? In the Sixties.

Feminism

It was during this period that the movement commonly called Feminism began to pick up momentum, especially with the publication of Betty Friedan's *The Feminine Mystique* in 1963. Its roots, of course, go back much earlier. Elizabeth Cady Stanton of Seneca Falls, New York, devoted her life to the cause of women's rights and organized the first Women's Rights Convention in 1848. She was especially outraged at the exclusion of women from the pastoral office in the church and pointedly said so in her *Declaration of Sentiments*, modeled after the Declaration of Independence. She published her *Women's Bible*, with its cunning commentary on texts she found demeaning to women, in 1895. In time her ideas took root in American society, and women began to be ordained as ministers in the major denominations in the 1970s (though Fundamentalist and Pentecostal groups had had them for years, Aimee Semple McPherson having been a nationally known figure). The Episcopal Church has designated July 20, the closing day of the first Women's Rights Convention, as an official day of commemoration for Stanton and three other nineteenth-century feminists: Amelia Jenks Bloomer, Sojourner Truth, and Harriet Tubman.

If Stanton struggled against the Church, other feminists, like Mary Malone, simply walked away from it. A prominent Roman Catholic theologian and former nun, Malone reached a crisis when she found she could no longer recite the Nicene Creed. Charles Colson notes: "Malone began searching for a faith that would accommodate her feminist beliefs. Like many other feminists, she ultimately embraced paganism." Paganism today is a word for the indigenous religions in pre-Christian Europe. More on this later. Its appeal to feminists seems to be that it centers in goddess-worship and nature. "Goddess spirituality has started to spread out across the world as women, dissatisfied with a male god, seek out a female one," says Kelly McElveen. If women are seeking power, this is certainly the way. The goddess is a symbol of powerful and independent femininity. You begin by worshiping the goddess and in the end you become a goddess yourself. Of course deities demand sacrifice. And what else is an abortion but the blood sacrifice of a living child to the pagan goddess?

Homosexuality

Years ago those who were homosexual stayed in the closet, keeping a low profile. No longer. Kids today get positive messages about homosexuality from society and see gays portrayed in a positive light by the media. Like Feminism, the Gay Rights Movement really took off in the Sixties. There was a place in New York called the Stonewall Bar, a watering hole for homosexual men. The cops would raid it routinely, but one day in 1969 one of the patrons kicked back, then another and another, and it escalated into what is now called the Stonewall Riot, a kind of Bastille Day for homosexuals. From there the Gay Rights Movement continued to mobilize and organize through the Seventies with increasing success. When the gay community was struck by the AIDS plague in the Eighties, it was able to elicit not the opprobrium of society but its sympathy. A modern Sodom and Gomorrah would qualify for federal disaster relief.

As with Feminism, there is an implicit paganism to homosexuality. St. Paul puts his finger on the problem when he analyzes the homosexuality in Roman culture. "God gave them over in the sinful desires of their hearts to sexual impurity for the degrading of their bodies with one another. They exchanged the truth of God for a lie, and worshiped and served created things rather than the Creator—who is forever praised. Amen" (Romans 1:24-25). In the old order of holy matrimony, the man says to the woman, "With my worldly goods I thee endow, with my body I thee worship." It means that there is a proper and God-pleasing sense of sacrifice and praise to the object of one's affections in marriage. But when a man gives this sacrifice and praise to a member of his own sex, it is craven idolatry. It is a violation of the First Commandment, which forbids worshiping any other god before the Lord. It is a perversion of the First Article of the Apostles' Creed, which summarizes the Bible's teaching on creation and the divinely established natural order of things, including marriage. Homosexuality is basically a theological problem. A heresy. It begins with false doctrine and ends with perverted behavior.

And, like pagan Feminism, its pagan homosexuality centers in the cult of death. That is the connection between sodomy and abortion. Both are acts of false worship—one praise and the other sacrifice. One is death at the point of contact; the other is death at the point of delivery.

Of course people defend their religious practices with great zeal. Among Protestants we are now fighting the so-called "worship wars," with one side advocating contemporary praise songs and the other traditional liturgy and hymns. But feminists and gays are struggling to preserve something that is essential to their religion, without which they would cease to exist. That is why the debates are so irrational and hysterical. Those who oppose abortion and sodomy on Christian grounds are trying to destroy a pagan rite.

Paganism

Feminism and homosexuality aside, no one can doubt that paganism has generally become more widespread in our society. The U.S. Army now has an officially recognized Wiccan circle at Ft. Hood, Texas. Not only fighters but thinkers are attracted to the ancient religion. David Abel reported on a pagan worship service of fifty students, held at the MIT chapel in Cambridge, Massachusetts. Its attraction, he says, is to students and academics who have rejected traditional Western monotheistic religions such as Christianity and Judaism but need some form of spirituality. Paganism, or its more organized traditional form called Wicca (not to be confused with witchcraft), fits nicely with the environmentalism, feminism, and multiculturalism popular on campuses. Interestingly, the ancient religion is facilitated by modern technology as the Internet helps seekers find pagan groups and network with each other.

Wicca has no defined dogma, as does Christianity with its creeds and confessions. And since Wicca was practically extinguished during the Christian era, one cannot be certain that modern neopaganism is a true repristination of the old. Still, its outlines can be distinguished. It is polytheistic, admitting the worship of many gods. It is natural, focusing on reverence for nature, season, and bodily rhythms. For women pagans, the moon and its parallel with the monthly menstrual cycle assumes great importance. Modern Wiccans talk about coming out of the "broom closet." But Wicca is nature worship, not Satan worship. Its witches cast spells and try to tune in to earth-generated energy fields, as happened in the 1980s with the "Harmonic Convergence" at Sedona, Arizona, and other vortex sites.

This religion has been around since the dawn of time. Indeed, some attribute it to Lilith, the legendary first wife of Adam, who became too powerful and independent and was expelled from the Garden of Eden in favor of the more compliant and submissive Eve. If Christians had to struggle against paganism in Europe, the Israelites had to do the same in Palestine before them. The Canaanites were notorious for their goddess-centered fertility cults, and the catalogue of their hair-raising iniquities is written in Leviticus 18 (for those brave enough to read it). In judgment against them, God brought a desert-hardened army of Israelites across the Jordan to destroy them.

Mythology

The Greeks and Romans were technically not pagans. As we saw earlier, the term *pagan* comes from the Latin for "country." Those ancient cultures were urbane and sophisticated. Their pantheon consisted of mythical gods and goddesses embodying principles of nature and human conduct. Zeus/Jupiter was the chief god, always chasing after some pretty mortal or other. Ares/Mars was the god of war, whose mistress was Aphrodite/Venus, the goddess of love. Hermes/Mercury was the messenger god. His name is encoded in the term *hermeneutics*, the study of the principles of biblical interpretation. In the sophisticated Greco-Roman culture, men made sacrifices to these gods and held festivals, but they did not relate to them the same way we do with Christ.

The Hindu pantheon is not unlike that of the Greeks. Indra, the supreme Hindu deity, is similar to Zeus, sky-god and ruler of the other gods. Hera, wife of Zeus, corresponds to Uma, female mother goddess of the Hindus. It is now known that both Greek and Hindu civilizations stem from a common root. Around 1,500 B.C. the Aryan people of central Asia began to migrate. One group successfully invaded India; the other conquered Greece. Both became the dominant cultural groups in their respective regions. The Aryans in India created the caste system (with themselves at the apex, of course), while the Aryans in Greece established systems of thought that continue to mold Western civilization. Parallels between Sanskrit and Western tongues point to the common origins of what is now called the Indo-European family of languages.

Through myth, then, there is access to an easy bridge between Eastern and Western thought. And, as Joseph Campbell taught, modern man, schooled in rationalism and the limitations of the scientific method, has a deep need for the numinous mode of thought that is accessible only through myth and the associated arts of music and poetry. More recently, poet Robert Bly has explored the benefits of pagan ritual for modern men.

Norse mythology is of a completely different sort, more austere and forbidding, a world of northernness completely fascinating to Richard Wagner and C. S. Lewis alike. It stems from a completely different root than the Indo-European system. Odin, or Wotan, was chief of the gods, as was Zeus/Indra. From his name is derived our *Wednesday. Thursday* comes from Thor, the god of thunder. Frigg was Odin's wife, paralleling Hera/Uma. One key difference is that there is an eschatology in Norse mythology that is different from that of the Greek/Hindu systems. Hindu mythology sees an almost endless cycle of ends and beginnings for the world; the Greek gods and the earth simply continue on forever. Norse mythology anticipates a climactic final battle, called *Ragnarok,* between the gods and the giants. All deities are killed, the earth is destroyed by fire, the human race is recreated, and a new and better world is born.

Eschatology and Evolution

What sometimes escapes observers of the new spirituality is that it, too, has a kind of implicit eschatology. It is not cataclysmic like the Norse, however. It is more similar to the postmillennial eschatology that pervades Roman Catholic and liberal Protestant theology. This, you recall, is the idea that man will create a new and better world, a thousand-year reign of peace and justice at the end of which Christ will come. The secular version of this is found in liberal or Socialist political thought, where man strives to create a better world but omits the Second Coming. In spiritual terms, the eponymous "new age" is the Age of Aquarius, a sort of millennium of peace and harmony that is coming about after a period of wars and strife. In one sense, this is supposed to be coming upon us as a manifestation of astrological destiny. In another sense, it is being deliberately formed by the actions of an advance guard of more highly-evolved human beings.

Which brings us to the parallels between mythology and science. Long ago C. S. Lewis pointed out how the idea of man evolving from lower life-forms originated in Egyptian mythology and found its way through the Greek poets into Western thought. Darwin's genius was to provide supposedly scientific proof for an idea that was already well-established among the poets and philosophers. Of course, if man evolved from lower life-forms, then he must even now be evolving into something higher. Hence the appeal of Catholic author Teilhard de Chardin's mystical science to New Agers. New Age maven Marilyn Ferguson sees her Aquarian Conspirators as new products of human evolution—not physically but spiritually.

Native American Spirituality

The new spirituality borrows from all systems of mythology and has much admiration for the Native American. Dominant among these was the civilization of the Aztecs, which flourished in Central America from the 1300s until the conquest by Cortez in 1521. This religious system had at its core a rite of human sacrifice in which war captives were laid on a stone altar and had their beating hearts cut out and eaten by priests. (Cortez—good Catholic that he was—put a stop to this right away.) Accordingly, the Aztecs developed a complex mythology, incorporating elements from their own religion plus those of previous civilizations as well as conquered peoples. New Age belief has a similar kind of religious syncretism—a capacity to assimilate and embrace bits and pieces of all different kinds of religious motifs, no matter how contradictory. One will use a crystal for meditation, employ channeling, incorporate some yoga, delve into Native American spirituality, and so on.

Ferguson describes the unification process of the New Age. Scientists trained in logic now appreciate meditation and mysticism from the East. Businessmen weaned on the vinegar of competition now discover the benefits of cooperation and attend New-Age seminars at company expense. Old-time conservationists who used to worry about contour plowing evolve into ecologists who save whales and hug trees. Teachers who once drubbed the Three Rs into little skulls become agents of social change. Women formerly content to be housewives now go out and get tough and get rich. Men who ate nails for breakfast now get in touch with their sensitive feminine side. Politicians who wielded raw power find common ground with the opposition through a blurring of party distinctions. And as leaders in these various fields find each other and begin to communicate, says Ferguson, "a leaderless but powerful network is working to bring about radical change in the U.S." (23). Not that there haven't already been networks of religiously-minded men at work in America for a long time.

The Lodge

Those who have read Tolstoy's *War and Peace* will recall that much of the backdrop centered around the sinister machinations of a mysterious new secret organization that was making inroads into the leadership of eighteenth-century European society—the Masonic Lodge. The lodge in America today is pervasive but seemingly benign, something out of an older generation of AmVets and Jaycees, an institution held up to gentle parody in *Amos 'n Andy's* Mystic Knights of the Sea and the Loyal Order of the Raccoon on *The Honeymooners*. So common was lodge membership that the saying arose down South, "To get elected you have to be a Mason, a Methodist, and a Democrat."

There's some truth to this, of course. And while there is no fundamental conflict between affiliating with a church and a political party—President Eisenhower took instruction and joined the Presbyterian Church while in office—theologically stricter denominations have always opposed the lodges. Public disclaimers to the contrary, the lodges are far more than social clubs and a place where you can get a drink on Sunday. As Dr. Phillip Lochhaas, former Director of the LCMS Commission on Organizations, has pointed out, "All lodges are essentially religious organizations which deny the divinity of Christ." These groups, from the Masons to the Moose, promote a there-is-only-one-God-but-many-paths-to-Him kind of universalism. A viewpoint, one notes immediately, that is firmly embraced by the new spirituality.

Cults

It would be impossible of course to trace a historical connection between the lodges, which began with the Masons in the eighteenth century, and the many cults and sects that began to arise in America in the nineteenth century, or the new spirituality in the twentieth. (Although Joseph Smith became a Mason in Nauvoo, Illinois, and patterned Mormon temple rites after Masonic ceremonies.) At the same time one is struck by how much all of these disparate groups have in common. It is as if they were all different dishes coming out of one kitchen with the same cook.

The Mormons, like the Muslims, believe that divine revelation did not end with Scripture, but that there would be future revelations through new prophets. The Masons, like the Jehovah's Witnesses, reject the idea of eternal punishment in hell for unrepentant sinners. The New Agers, like the Christian Scientists, maintain that suffering is illusion and affirm the power of the human mind to bring about healing. And above all, none of them accept what Christ says about Himself: "I and the Father are one" (John 10:30). The first principle of all heresy is false Christology—making Jesus either more or less than He really is. Once that false premise is established, the rest falls into place.

So while one cannot establish a causal lodge-cult-New Age link in all cases, still one can see points of commonality, a unified field of opinion on key questions. The apostasy from orthodox Christianity that set in with eighteenth-century Rationalism opened the way for the rise of the lodges, then the cults, and now today's new spirituality. Who's in the kitchen cooking all this up?

The Sixties

While Thoreau, Emerson, and the New England Transcendentalists of the nineteenth century, read Eastern philosophy, it seems clear that the Sixties opened the floodgate to this influence in America. As noted, each epoch seems to be marked by a symbolic event. For our purposes here I nominate the 1969 Woodstock music festival, universally known as a cultural icon but frequently misunderstood (see Figure 2, p. 48). Surface impressions notwithstanding, there was an underlying spiritual dimension to the counterculture. The agitators of the New Left, the antiwar protestors, and the civil rights activists got all the press in those days. They were demonstrating, making speeches, getting shot, doing things that made sensational copy for the papers and looked dramatic on the evening TV news. People naturally concluded that these political incursions were central to the cultural upheaval that was sweeping the nation. In time the Baby Boomers, whose sheer demographic size made the movements of the Sixties possible, matured and sat down at the table where decisions are made. What was the result? Conservative government and a business boom at home through the Eighties and Nineties, coupled with the fall of Communism overseas. The impetus of radical politics was not sustained. In fact, the first Boomer president, Bill Clinton, was a Democrat, but he antagonized the liberal base of his party by running on a moderate platform. In the 2000 election, both candidates—both Boomers—appealed to the political middle.

At the same time something very quiet but far more unsettling began to seep into our culture in a major way from Woodstock on, a major influx of alternative religious ideas, with a revival of Wicca, new strains of Eastern mysticism, Native American spirituality, home-grown mind control cults. . . . Even the Jesus Freaks had their day in the sun. Not that these things were unknown in America before. It's just that Woodstock opened the floodgates. Many of the hippies were into drugs, but not just for the purpose of getting stoned and escaping reality. Marijuana, an old ghetto drug, spread into the middle class. Mexican Indian peyote produced a high. Then LSD came along, and it seemed like there was an instant chemical shortcut to the enlightenment that Eastern mystics offered only through years of discipline and study. That quest was central to the Sixties drug culture. No one realized the danger at the time. Drugs have always been essential to pagan religious practice, a perception encoded in the etymology of the New Testament. Its word for "witchcraft" is the Greek *pharmakeia*, from which we get our word *pharmacy*. Of course in the Sixties, witchcraft, like drug use, was seen as something benign. Something different and fascinating.

Some of the Beat poets and writers of the Fifties such as Jack Kerouac, Allen Ginsberg, and Gary Snyder were influenced by Zen Buddhism. As the counterculture movement of the Sixties began to gather force, Ginsberg in particular became a kind of father figure to the younger writers. Bob Dylan, "the spokesman for his generation," had his picture taken with Ginsberg and several other Beat poets in front of Lawrence Ferlinghetti's City Lights Bookstore in San Francisco. Hindu sitar virtuoso Ravi Shankar gave concerts in the United States. Going the opposite direction, the Beatles traveled to India to study meditation with a famous guru, Maharishi Mahesh Yogi, the Founder of Transcendental Meditation (TM). Gurus by the score came to America to cash in on the fad, while kids by the thousands traveled to India in search of an illusive nirvana.

Much of the developing counterculture centered in San Francisco's Haight-Ashbury district, with the drug culture mixing with Eastern mysticism and influencing not only poetry as had the earlier Beatniks, but rock music. Psychedelic bands such as the Grateful Dead and Jefferson Airplane eschewed crass commercialism while selling millions of records and promoting a philosophy of peace, love, and naturalness. I myself happened to be in San Francisco during those years and can testify that the Sixties was more about religion than politics.

As time moved on, the drug culture got really ugly, as was inevitable, and countless young lives were destroyed by bad trips on LSD. But the religious impetus carried on into the Seventies. Guru-led American ashrams continued to flourish, while even more sinister mind control cults like those led by Charles Manson and Jim Jones and David Koresh sprang up and attracted adherents. But you had to join those; you had to make a commitment and become a member.

Then something unusual began to happen: The counterculture began to spread into the mainstream. As one guru, Ram Dass, said in 1979 with some amazement about those who were coming to hear him teach, "For the most part it's the middle class these days . . . where

I was working with a ten-year age span out of the alternative cultures five or six years ago, I'm now seeing a fifteen-year span out of the mainstream of society—what used to be called straight" (Ferguson, 365). Marilyn Ferguson, whose *The Aquarian Conspiracy* is considered the Bible of the New Age movement, notes how widespread this cultural change has become. Science, traditionally the domain of left-brain logic, began to explore the new, more mystical modes of knowledge. Teilhard de Chardin, like Merton a Roman Catholic mystic, was trained in science and put forth an argument for a new kind of evolution, one that would bring about an advance in consciousness and achieve the transformation of society. Here and there, more highly evolved minds—the New Agers—were springing up, a kind of advance guard preparing the way for the rest of mankind to follow. Heady stuff, if you're one of the chosen few. And if the husband and kids don't understand, well, sometimes you have to make tough choices and move on . . .

So now a new religious atmosphere has come to penetrate all levels of human enterprise in America—science, education, business, the military, the family. How will things look in the future? The classroom of the future will be more cooperative, less authoritarian. The workplace will be less rigid and more flexible, more harmonious and less competitive. Professional sports, already in decline, will continue to dwindle while the arts get bigger. In recent years there has been serious concern in the baseball world about whether the Montreal Expos, for example, will be able to stay in business. A few years ago the Cincinnati Reds were playing before crowds of 5,000. Meanwhile, papers reported attendance at city art museums increasing sharply, even among blue-collar people.

Men will be more emotional, women more autonomous. Children will be able to develop more naturally, without all of that bothersome parental authority that comes from patriarchal Christianity. And churches—Protestant and Catholic alike—will get along in a spirit of ecumenical cooperation, with a new and liberating understanding that there is at last only one God and many different paths to find Him. Old political animosities will diminish as conservatives and liberals move together in a new spirit of harmony. In time this rising tide of new consciousness will naturally result in the transformation of society, and the Age of Aquarius will truly come to pass. People will love one another and have a new understanding of things formerly thought to divide—superficial distinctions like race and culture. Tolerance will reign supreme—except of course for that irritating remnant of harsh, right-wing religious extremists who continue to insist on biblical standards of truth and conduct. Those people will be found guilty of hate crimes. They will have to be dealt with in no uncertain terms. Church and state will cooperate in the administration of justice.

Like a Beast from the Earth

All these ingredients in the roiling pot of our culture are slippery; it's hard to get a grip on them. We must turn to the Bible to find a metaphor, an image that will help us discern what might be happening in our civilization.

As the hinge of time swings to a new millennium, some are encouraged by possibilities for Christian renewal. Not long ago, at century's end, prominent Protestant Charles Colson quoted a prominent Catholic: "As we approach the new millennium, I am increasingly convinced that it can be, as Pope John Paul II says, a 'springtime for Christianity.' . . . The reason is simply that the postmodern age is imploding, crumbling in on itself." The postmodern age is indeed collapsing, but a consequent springtime for Christianity—as appealing as that might be—would not seem to correspond either to Scripture or to reality. At least not in the way Colson imagines. We have discussed the reality of changes in our culture. What does Scripture teach? Not a springtime for the Church, but an autumnal season of increasing storms while the last harvest is gathered in.

In the Revelation, St. John describes two beasts, one from the sea and one from the earth. The beast from the sea "was given power to make war against the saints and to conquer them" (Revelation 13:7). Here is a symbolic description of the exercise of force against the Church. The sea is a general symbol in Scripture for history, government, the temporal affairs of men—always agitated and turbulent, restless, stormy, but with a fixed limit beyond which it cannot go. David praises God "who stilled the roaring of the seas, the roaring of their waves, and the turmoil of the nations" (Psalm 65:7). Here David compares the seas to the nations. Certainly this beast is at work against God's holy people throughout the last days. Rome was against us in the beginning; then the Muslims attacked for centuries. The last century saw widespread opposition from Communist governments. Government-sponsored physical persecution continues today around the world, especially in Africa and China.

The beast from the earth is related to the beast from the sea: "Because of the signs he was given power to do on behalf of the first beast, he deceived the inhabitants of the earth" (Revelation 13:14). Here is described not force, but persuasion. This beast is likewise at work against God's people throughout the end times. As we have seen from a close look at the time of the apostles and Fathers, there *was* no golden age in the early Church. St. Paul contended with the Judaizers, St. John with the Gnostics. Marcion advanced a Gospel with no counterbalancing law to the early Church and drew many away from the truth. Our Nicene Creed was developed by the Fathers as a statement—indeed, a test—of orthodoxy against the Arian heresy that deemphasized the divinity of Christ. And so it has continued.

Robert Hoerber writes, "The beast out of the earth . . . symbolizes apostate religion, as 13:1-10 refers to hostile civil government. . . . In a broader sense this beast represents all doctrine which undermines the gospel and promotes the purposes of the devil" (CSSB, 1962). Taking the Greek word for "beast" [*thére*], I have coined the term *Therian* to describe the advance of false religion that we are seeing in our time. The New Age movement is a beginning. A century or two ago it might have been a passing fad, a trend that would end up as a footnote in a theological textbook. Something much broader and deeper is now emerging.

Christianity dominated Western civilization for a long Ideational period, through the Middle Ages and beyond. There followed a Sensate period—the Modern—in which secular values predominated and Christianity began to decline. This Sensate culture in turn began to break down in the nineteenth and twentieth centuries, accompanied by a marked increase in government-backed persecution of the Church. What then comes after Postmodernism? The Therian Age; that is, an Ideational phase of Western—perhaps world—civilization that is innately religious but hostile to Christianity. Or, perhaps even worse, a dominant but false Christian church that brings all of its forces to bear against the truth of God's Word.

9

What Israel Should Do

We have essayed in these pages to understand the times in which we live, in the spirit of the men who joined David ("men of Issachar, who understood the times and knew what Israel should do," 1 Chronicles 12:32). Taking a look at the big picture, we have seen that there are cultural dynamics at work in our civilization, just as there are seasons in nature. Over the course of centuries there has been a very slow modulation between Sensate and Ideational phases, like between Winter and Summer. There have been Transitional times in between, partly hot and partly cold, with a cultural mixture of material and spiritual elements. It remains now to sum things up, take a look at the state of the Church today, and draw out implications for future events and future action. As the writer of Chronicles put it, what Israel—God's people, the Church—should do.

Weakened Christianity

Of great concern to all must be the weakened state in which Christianity finds itself today, especially as it faces the challenge of a surging new Ideational culture or Therian Age. The collapse of medieval Christian culture followed by the devastating effects of secular modern movements such as Rationalism and Romanticism have taken a tremendous toll on the vitality of the Church.

The medieval church in the West, with all its problems, was at least a unified entity. From one end of Europe to the other, one could attend church and hear the same message and experience the same worship service. Catholics accuse Protestants of breaking up this unity. This is true, in a sense. Luther never wanted to split from Rome; he just wanted his church to adopt reasonable measures of positive change. But the pope set his face against reform and excommunicated Luther. So the reformer and his followers were forced to organize separately. In essence the blame for the Protestant/Catholic split can be laid at the foot of the pope.

But once the splitting started, like a crack in the windshield of your car, it just continued to progress and move in unexpected, crazy directions. First there were Lutherans, then came the Zwinglians and the Calvinists. The Baptists arose, and after a time the Methodists and their cousins the Pentecostals. As might have been expected, the groups themselves began to split. In America today among Lutherans there are the Lutheran Church-Missouri Synod (LCMS), the Evangelical Lutheran Church in America (ELCA), the Wisconsin Evangelical Lutheran Synod (WELS), to name but three major denominations, none of which is in fellowship with any of the others, to say nothing of the many small ultraconservative Lutheran groups. So the Protestants are fragmented within themselves.

Not that things are any better among the Catholics. In one place there are gun-toting Marxist priests, in another those who cling to the Latin mass. Here there are Catholic monks holding joint meditation sessions with their Buddhist counterparts, and over there are primitive groups that are essentially pagan. While justification by faith is taught here and there in the Roman Catholic Church, the main emphasis is still salvation by works. The practical result is an emphasis on Law over the Gospel. The whole structure is held together primarily by the authority of the pope, not by any doctrinal consensus. Internally, the Catholics are as fragmented as the Protestants.

Along with the upheavals of the Reformation came the religious wars of the sixteenth and seventeenth centuries. In Europe it was Catholic against Lutheran as the pope tried to stamp out the new "heresy" by force, just as the Eastern church had attempted to do in the past during its struggle with the Monophysites. In England it was Puritan against Anglican, with Cromwell fighting to establish a more righteous civil order in this present world. The result was that by mid-seventeenth century many people were sick of fighting and to some degree sick of the Christian religion that had brought about the fighting. We Christians have a lot to repent of in this respect. In truth, one can sympathize with secular liberal thinkers who fear the rise of conservative Christian involvement in politics. They imagine—and with good cause—that if we gained power we'd burn our opponents (like them) at the stake.

This state of affairs is naturally troubling to any thinking Christian, whether Protestant or Catholic. Such a broken-up Christianity barely held off the Turks at the Battle of Vienna in 1530 and was ill-prepared to defend itself against the rising power of secular thought in the philosophy and science of the seventeenth century and beyond. Historians have noted that the effect of the Enlightenment in Europe in the eighteenth century was to reduce church attendance by 90 percent—a falling away from which the church has never recovered.

To further complicate matters, optimistic secularism—which thought it could provide an alternative to religion—came to a dead stop with World War I. In its aftermath there were attempts to build unity. Woodrow Wilson established the League of Nations to bring about political harmony in the secular arena. Likewise, church leaders in the Twenties began meetings to further unity among Christian denominations. It was widely felt that a unified church could have prevented the Great War and if now created might prevent further devastation. The result was the Ecumenical Movement, in which Protestant denominations worked toward external unity. Today (liberal) Presbyterians, Lutherans, and Episcopalians can commune at each other's altars and share pastors with each other's pulpits, even though they have no substantial doctrinal agreement and probably never will.

In Europe after the Peace of Westphalia (1648), spiritual jurisdictions coincided with the political. The Lutherans held northern Germany, the Calvinists Geneva, the Catholics Italy, and so forth. In America there were no such geographic boundaries. Instead there were confessional boundaries that one dared not cross. You went to your Baptist church but did not commune at the altar of the Methodist church across the street. And heaven help you if you got engaged to someone from a different denomination and Grandma found out about it. The border was in your mind.

The ecumenical movement has largely done away with this ecclesiastical geography. Christians of different denominations get along better on a local level, and there is more cooperation on an official level. Thankfully there are no religious wars in this country. But at the same time the confessional hedges have been broken down. Few take theology seriously anymore. As with New Agers, so with Christians: People retain completely contradictory beliefs. A Catholic in America today may submit to the pope but embrace birth control and abortion, both of which are against the teachings of Rome. Recently this was the public and defiant position of Pennsylvania Governor Tom Ridge (a Republican), despite the opprobrium of his bishop. By the same token other Catholics might embrace elements of Marxism or Eastern mysticism. And in the same way a Protestant, under the rubric of the priesthood of the individual believer, might believe that he has had visits and messages from angels while upholding the sufficiency of Scripture; he might deny the real presence of Christ in the Lord's Supper, yet presume to commune at the altar of a church where this is taught. Official church relations and theological distinctives are swept aside, and each man becomes a denomination unto himself.

To make matters worse, modern schools of theology have undermined the faith once delivered to the saints. The rise of Sensate secularism apart from the Church soon had its effect on the Church. Rationalism swept from Germany to England to America in the eighteenth century, gaining influence in the universities, and from the universities to the seminaries, and from the seminaries to the pulpits. Theologians—and soon pastors—came to question the inerrancy of the Bible, analyzing it as just another ancient document. From there it was only a short step to questioning the miracles in the Bible; the historicity of Jonah and the virgin birth came under close scrutiny. Ultimately belief in the Resurrection and finally the existence of Christ Himself became matters for debate. Of course it is the Gospel that is always and ultimately at issue. Sermons began to contain less and less of it. Instead of proclaiming that God raised Christ from the grave, pastors in Germany lectured their parishioners on better methods by which they could raise potatoes from the earth.

Romanticism, with its emphasis on subjectivity, soon found a voice in theology with the thought of Friedrich Schleiermacher (1768-1834). Reacting against the Enlightenment (not to mention biblical theology), Schleiermacher put forth the concept of a "taste and feeling for the infinite" (LC, 700). The perception of the individual now took center stage, with an emphasis on the *idea* of the Church, the *idea* of redemption. Today one may safely assert that most people in the churches depend more upon their own inner feelings than upon an objective truth outside of themselves.

Add to this the continued influence of the old heresies. Marcion came and went in the second century, but everywhere people want love, love, love and would be horrified to hear a sermon describing Christ as a righteous judge who will send the wicked into eternal damnation. Montanus flourished in the third century; yet on every block there is a preacher spouting that the Lord gave him a word

about the imminence of the Second Coming. Nothing about the forgiveness of sins, though. Arius was condemned in the fourth century,
but a perceptive person can see everywhere a de-emphasis on the
divinity of Christ. Jesus is depicted in popular church art as smiling,
athletic, and popular. Never mind that this is the Son of God, begotten before all worlds. Pelagius was rejected in the fifth century, but
any pastor working in the vineyard knows that the average parish-
ioner thinks he will go to heaven because he was sincere and tried
to be good. With that outlook, Jesus' crucifixion was completely
unnecessary.

In a Transitional period like the twentieth century and its aftermath, the atmosphere of the culture is inhaled by Christians like
radon gas. They can't see it or smell it, but they are absorbing the
deadly substance anyway. It is a part of their lives even though they
are unaware of it.

The Sensate tendency toward the sensual and the immorally sexual was emerging in the conduct of "advanced" people and artists
such as Oscar Wilde and the Bloomsbury Group in the late nineteenth
and early twentieth centuries and continued downward and outward
through all levels of society. We commonly look to the Sixties and
blame the Baby Boomers for the change in mores. In reality, it was our
grandparents in the Roaring Twenties who started the sexual revolution. Now it is affecting even those who are in the world but not supposed to be of it. Today the overall clergy divorce rate is about the
same as society in general. This was unheard of a century ago, and
may be a century hence.

Along with the poets' concentration on low persons and distaste-
ful behavior, there has been a corresponding coarsening of social inter-
course. There is less courtesy on the roadways than there used to be.
The rate of illegitimate births among the predominantly middle-class
white population—our largest demographic group—is now approaching that of poor blacks, even as the black middle class grows by leaps
and bounds. By the same token, all surveys indicate a rising tide of

rudeness among even Christian people, and congregational governing boards routinely treat the man of God in their midst with disrespect.

Everybody likes to disdain the poet who thinks of himself as somebody special, separate from ordinary society and exempt from its mores, one who writes difficult verse that nobody can understand. Yet at the same time we think nothing of being in contact with the computer nerd who speaks and writes nothing but totally incomprehensible gobbledygook.

Our grandparents lived in ethnic urban neighborhoods like the brawny, vibrant "Chicago" of which Carl Sandburg sang. As the cities changed and deteriorated after World War II, our parents escaped to the suburbs, not one inch of which has ever inspired a poem. Now we are living in the complacent exurbs—the same place to which middle-class blacks are moving to get away from underclass urban blacks, little thinking that the death of the head means the death of the limbs as well. Moreover, as the massacre of students at Columbine High School in Littleton, Colorado, showed the nation, now even the complacent suburbs are no longer safe. And the death of the city has been portrayed by the poets for a long time now. It's all of a piece—the movement of thought and conduct from the poets to the streets.

These trends are well-established in our society and will continue for some time. There remain with us residual influences from all eras of our civilization, but these postmodern modes of thought and behavior are dominant today, along with the new religious currents of the Therian Age. And on it goes. The enemy grows in unity and strength, while we squabble amongst ourselves and become weaker by the day.

A New Rome

At the same time that the Christian religion seems to be weakening overall, the Roman Catholic Church shows signs of renewed strength. Rome had seemed hopelessly out of tune with the times by mid-twentieth century. Then Pope John XXIII initiated the Second Vatican

Council (1963-1965), which opened the ecumenical door and called observers from other denominations—even those formerly condemned as heretics—"separated brethren." Many had been suspicious of Rome because of its failure to oppose Hitler and Mussolini during World War II. Then in 1979 the Polish Pope, John Paul II, came to power. He confronted Communism and helped to hasten its eventual downfall.

Known for dogmatic inflexibility, Rome has at the same time shown a remarkable capacity for theological diversity and inclusiveness. For example, Robert Lentz is a contemporary painter who works in the iconic style (see Figure 3, p. 171). Ancient Christian artists in the Eastern church developed the *icon*, from the Greek word for "image." An icon is a highly stylized picture of Christ or a saint in a formal pose and with a golden halo. These icons are held in almost sacramental reverence by the faithful; it was taught that by contemplating the icon, one could come closer to God. While the ancient artists focused on Christ and the apostles, Lentz has portrayed more contemporary figures such as Elizabeth Cady Stanton, Martin Luther King, and Harvey Milk. He gives the message that these are our living saints.

One of his most interesting icons is of the Trappist monk, Thomas Merton. Merton was a product of the Western church, having lived most of his religious life at a monastery in Kentucky. As befits the iconic style, Merton has a golden halo. His right hand is raised to impart a blessing. But Merton was a Catholic who was drawn to the spirituality of Oriental religions. He held joint meditation sessions with monks from the Buddhist tradition. So Lentz portrays Merton sitting in the lotus position like the Buddha, with bamboo in the background. His flowing robes seem Oriental, but there is a Cistercian cowl—typical of Western monastic garb—at the shoulders. The Greek words on either side of the head say, "Holy Thomas." A modern Catholic monk is portrayed as a saint in Buddhist mystic attire. In sum, East meets West, and one is sanctified by the other. Lentz says of Merton, "He pointed the way for Western Christians in this time of profound cultural change."

Figure 3:
Thomas Merton by Robert Lentz

Merton was not alone in his quest for integration. One of his notable predecessors was Bede Griffiths, a British Benedictine monk who, like many Englishmen, became fascinated by the culture and religion of the prize colony, India. In the course of a very long life, Griffiths became a student of Hinduism and author of many books on the subject of the harmony between Christianity and the Hindu religion. In his autobiography, *The Golden String*, he describes his inner spiritual journey and its practical application. He eventually went to live in India, where he established a Christian-Hindu ashram.

It is important to note that these are not aberrations in the Catholic church. The mysticism of Merton and Griffiths flows out of the center of their religion. Even the Catholic church of the Middle Ages held pagan philosophers in high esteem. Aquinas certainly admired Aristotle and tried to harmonize his philosophy with Christian theology. Virtuous pagans who did not actively oppose the Gospel or who were ignorant of it had been consigned to a higher region of the underworld. Old paintings depict them being liberated by Christ along with Old Testament saints in the Harrowing of Hell. The worship of St. Mary is encoded paganism. More recently Catholic theologian Hans Küng asserted, "If a pagan surrenders himself in faith, in some obscure but real way, to the one true God in Jesus Christ, of whom he is perhaps only dimly aware under a hundred concealing veils, and if he then shows forth this faith in works of love, then he can be saved" (83). Küng was writing just before Vatican II. The theological tendency he represents appeared in the statements of *Lumen Gentium* ("light of the Gentiles"), one of the major documents produced by Vatican II.

Gottfried Martens noted the "universalism of salvation, as proclaimed by *Lumen Gentium*, which promises salvation also outside the church, also without Baptism and repentance, and declares that even pagans can enter heaven, if they have led an orderly life" (214). After Vatican II, Pope Paul VI visited Hindu and Muslim countries to great public acclaim and the approval of notable thinkers such as Arnold Toynbee. Admittedly, in later years the liberal and controversial Küng often crossed swords with the more conservative Pope John Paul II, but Küng does in fact represent a definite stream of thought in Catholicism that must be taken into account in any analysis of the current state of the Church. As Sasse asked, "Does it not belong to the nature of the Roman Catholic Church to be so comprehensive as to have a place for all partial truths?"

We have noted the threats to the Gospel from Islam and the New Age movement. We have seen the continuation of ancient heresies in contemporary Protestantism. We have observed the general tendency of Western civilization toward a new religious cultural mode. What we must keep in mind is the potential of the church of Rome to absorb and amalgamate all of these religious strains while claiming supremacy over all Christendom—indeed, spiritual and secular supremacy over all the world. This has always been the claim of the pope; it is also the underlying tendency and would be the logical outcome of the Ecumenical Movement. Ecumenism means "back to Rome."

I may be wrong. I hope I'm wrong. My prayer—like Luther's—is that the pope will correct the abuses of the past, repent of his false teachings, and preach the Gospel of Jesus Christ in all its articles on the basis of Scripture alone. He could be by far the greatest agent for genuine Christian revival. Imagine the potential for evangelism there could be with a Roman Catholic Church—one billion strong—freed from the shackles of medieval superstition, a church in which everyone studied the Bible, where everyone pursued true faith and not false works-righteousness, where every man witnessed to his neighbor.

But I fear it is not to be. As I write, Pope John Paul II is in declining health, and speculation is running high as to who might be his successor. The current pope represents the more conservative end of the theological spectrum in Rome (even though he has reaffirmed the compatibility of evolution with Catholic dogma); but the liberal forces that surfaced with figures like Griffiths and Merton and Küng have not gone away. Another John XXIII could bring them quickly back into power. Imagine the potential for destruction from a Roman Catholic Church freed from the shackles of biblical theology, a church in which everyone contemplated Zen koans, where everyone believed everything, no matter how contradictory, and where every man let his neighbor find an alternative path to spirituality.

In a Therian Age such a revitalized Rome would ratify paganism by declaring Mary co-redemptrix. It would further honor the Blessed Virgin by admitting women to the priesthood. It would succeed in rapprochement with liberal Protestantism. It would continue to absorb and promulgate the spiritual mysticism of Asia, a stream that now has a separate existence in the New Age movement. It would preside over the demolition of the wall of separation between church and state. As in the Middle Ages, there would be no philosophical or practical distinction between religion and culture, no barrier to the expression of that essentially religious culture in the institutions of education, law, and government. And as the Eastern Roman church/state gave no quarter to heretics, an ascendant Western Roman church/state would not tolerate that irritating remnant of true Christianity.

Against the Tide

One wonders how the Church should respond to larger cultural trends at work in society. Sorokin used the term "unintegrated opposite principle" to describe a phenomenon he had observed in which there are always latent Sensate forces present in an Ideational culture and vice versa. It seems to me, however, that the Church can and should be in the world as a constant unintegrated opposite principle. Whatever the prevailing trend is, there is something in biblical Christianity to offset it. In a Sensate age the Church emphasizes spiritual things. It told both Romans and Moderns to abstain from worldly lusts and set their minds on things above. In a Transitional period like the twentieth century where everything is in rapid flux, the Church offers stability, tradition, continuity with the past, and confidence toward the future. This sense of tradition is precisely the appeal of Eastern Orthodoxy to many Evangelicals today, even though they have had to sacrifice the Scripture principle to get it.

Our culture is moving into a new Ideational phase—the Therian Age. Even so, currents of thought from the past remain influential. The challenge now is to counterbalance the continuing arrogance of residual Rationalism with an emphasis on the legitimately supernatural elements of the faith such as miracles, mysteries, and the virgin birth. At the same time true Christianity will oppose the lingering subjectivism of Romanticism with an emphasis on the tangible elements of the faith such as Baptism, the Lord's Supper, and forensic justification. The

challenge furthermore is to find a local congregation where these balances are preserved: formal worship that is inspiring, passionate
Gospel preaching that is doctrinally sound, and Christian fellowship
that is warm but calls one to accountability.

The truth of the Gospel is often expressed in paradox: The last
shall be first; he who loses his life will find it. Confronted with theological tensions, church bodies have often resolved toward one pole or
the other. Liberals are full of love but have no solid basis for theology.
Conservatives have sound doctrine, but their hearts are full of envy and
hate. The charge might be made that the Roman Catholic Church has
emphasized the objective aspects of the Christian faith at the expense
of the subjective—rote ritual over personal faith, while the Evangelical
denominations have emphasized the subjective at the expense of the
objective—a personal relationship with Christ at the expense of liturgy.
Nevertheless there are congregations and denominations where the
ancient balances between the objective and subjective are preserved.

In a Therian Age the Church also offers counterbalance from its
reservoir of scriptural teaching and practice. The tendency of the spirit
of the age will be for people to become enthusiastic, superspiritual,
fanatical, disconnected from the world, floating up higher and higher
like a balloon without a string. To this the Church brings its theology
of the Incarnation. God comes down into this world and takes an
active role in the affairs of mankind. In the beginning God created the
heavens and the earth. He *made* Adam from the dust of the earth—
the Hebrew connotes the image of a sculptor working with clay,
sleeves rolled up and hands dirty. In His mercy He fashioned garments
for the poor sinners Adam and Eve. In His wrath He destroyed the first
world by water.

He loved the world so much that He sent His only-begotten Son,
Jesus Christ, so that whoever believes in Him will not perish but have
eternal life. God sent Him to us; we were not able to go up to heaven
and bring Him down. We would have made Him a worldly king, but
instead Jesus suffered and died on the cross. We offered our paltry good

works to God in payment for our sins, but Jesus gave His sinless body. In Him we have forgiveness of sins. He was named *Immanuel*, which means, "God with us." He comes to us; we do not go to Him. He ascended into heaven but remains with us. He is present wherever two or three are gathered together. He is present wherever the Word of God is taught in its truth and purity. He is present wherever someone gives a cup of cold water to a prophet. He is present in the poor, in the oppressed, in the least and forgotten of the world. He is present in works of mercy. He is really and truly present in the Sacraments of Baptism and Holy Communion. It is these concrete realities that the Church puts forward in a superspiritual time.

The Incarnation of Christ validates the arts in the Church. As the Incarnation is God becoming flesh, art is the materialization of an idea. In Christ, we have a man made of flesh and bone; not a ghost, but someone real who walked among us full of grace and truth. Likewise in the Sacraments of Baptism and Holy Communion we have God coming to us in the plain simple elements of water, of bread and wine. In a lesser way, art is incarnational. It *embodies* a concept. Johann Sebastian Bach, whose music is currently in revival (especially in Japan), was called "the Fifth Evangelist" because of the deep theological content of his work. The poets George Herbert and John Donne expressed the Christian faith in words. Rembrandt used the medium of paint and canvas to communicate the Christian religion. Today the call goes out to sanctified Christian young people to take up careers in the arts, and for Christian congregations and institutions to support them. As apologetics was well-suited to an age of reason, the arts will be well-suited to communicate the faith in this Therian Age when spiritual things and imagination are highly prized. We have seen the upswing of religious interest in erstwhile secular poets. As noted, there are increasing stirrings among God's people in this area as well. Scott Cairns notes "the body of American poetry's . . . remarkable transformation over the past decade—a decade which has seen a widespread return of religious typology, sacramental trope, and a relatively unselfconscious metaphysical speculation. . . . In

the span of a few years, we have witnessed a great increase—poets of
faith have grown in accomplishment, writing better poems, and already
accomplished poets have discovered a path to faith" (62).

If *Immanuel* means "God with us," its opposite is *enthusiasm*,
which means "God in us." As previously noted, it is the tendency in
every man to trust his inner religious feelings and attribute them to
God. This has been around since the dawn of time. According to
Luther, "Enthusiasm clings to Adam and his descendants from the
beginning to the end of the world . . . and it is the source, strength and
power of all heresy, including that of the papacy and Moham-
medanism" (Tappert, 313). On an individual basis, it means that people hold mutually contradictory beliefs based on nothing. This
tendency will be even more pronounced in the Therian Age. How
should the Church respond to it?

The Church has always had marvelous theological resources at its
fingertips. First of course is the Bible. Congregations everywhere
should offer solid Bible study programs for all ages. Give the youth a
topic on sex or drugs or rock 'n' roll once in a while, but by all means
get them into Romans. Find ways to teach the people to read the Bible
on their own. And pastors should preach biblical sermons. That
means studying Greek and Hebrew and doing the exegesis on a new
text every week. That means putting aside cozy little self-help chats
and telling people what the Bible says. The Bible is all about Jesus
Christ, and *every* sermon should make a clear proclamation of His
saving death and resurrection.

The Bible, however, can be misinterpreted. An enthusiast like
Muhammad can claim pure revelation from God apart from any written text. But an enthusiast like the Christian heretic Marcion knew his
Bible backwards and forwards. He just chose to interpret it in his own
way. In Bible classes pastors encourage people to do the same by asking, "What does this Bible verse mean *to you*?" Because of the constant
threat of heresy and in response to it, the Church has produced creeds,
or statements of belief, that define the essential teaching of the Bible.

There are three basic creeds that every Christian should know and every congregation should study on a regular basis. *The Apostles' Creed* was the catechism of the early church. Anyone wanting to be baptized had to know it well. This creed defines the Godhead as being comprised of the Father/Creator, the Son/Redeemer, and the Holy Spirit/Sanctifier. *The Nicene Creed* is Trinitarian in structure like the *Apostles'* but concentrates on Christological formulations in the Second Article. It was written to expound what the Bible teaches about the nature and work of Jesus Christ. Its wording was designed to repudiate the false teaching of the heretic Arius. These creeds were written in Greek. The great Latin creed of the Church is *the Athanasian Creed* (which, unfortunately, the Eastern Orthodox churches reject). It developed in France in the sixth century and goes into detail about the three persons of the Holy Trinity. In liturgical churches it is read on Trinity Sunday.

In addition to these, most church bodies (even Baptists) have *confessions*, doctrinal statements to which all members must adhere. The Lutheran Church has the *Augsburg Confession* and other doctrinal writings in the *Book of Concord*. The Presbyterian Church has the *Westminster Confession*. The Episcopalian Church has the *Thirty-nine Articles*. In the Therian Age, when people want to fly off in every spiritual direction at once, pastors owe it to their people to give them a solid foundation of dogma. Denominational publishing houses usually carry study guides on these doctrinal writings, suitable for small group or Sunday morning class study.

A third characteristic of the Therian Age will be complexity. Something like this is already in place when, as mentioned above, people hold contradictory beliefs. The spiritual world of someone like that is as complicated as the life of a man who has two wives. You try to please one, but what you do upsets the other, and vice versa, until you find yourself spinning in circles not knowing what to do. So it is with Therian man. He believes in reincarnation, but he is a member of a church whose pastor preaches about the Last Judgment. This creates dissonance. He goes to work on Monday and becomes an aggressive businessman. Yet he knows the Bible teaches honesty and compassion. More dissonance. Turn, turn, turn. In addition, congregations themselves try to become bigger and bigger and more and more complex as they try to provide something for everyone, like a mall.

Over against this trend the Church offers *simplicity*. There is something real about the Christian faith, something small and essential that you can carry in your pocket. Yet there always seems to be enough of it to pass around. We build big, fancy houses of worship to surround a pretty humble meal of bread and wine. We construct enormously complicated systems of dogmatic theology to describe our friendship with a man—the Last Man, the God-man, the Christ. If we keep these simple things in mind, we will provide healing for tangled-up people living in a too-complex, hurry-up world. In contrast to the degradation of marriage in our world, we find a way by God's grace to keep our covenants. Where there is coarseness and vulgarity around us, we cultivate manners. (Indeed, the Geneva Bible, which antedated the King James Version of 1611, translated Ephesians 4:32, "Be ye *courteous* to one another.") In this regard there may yet come a trend back toward the small, neighborhood congregation where everybody knows everybody. And as an antidote to the increased professionalism and commercialism that has taken over the arts, we can still bake our own. You look at the choir on Sunday morning and say, "There's Donna who cuts my hair. That's Joe who sells insurance." And that man in the pulpit, he is your local poet, the man of words who tells your epic at ceremonial functions and keeps your history. To him let there be all the honor that is traditionally reserved for the poet in our culture.

Siege Warfare

I have spoken of this new Ideational phase of Western civilization as the Therian Age, taking the term from the description in Revelation of the beast from the earth. "Paganism is always tolerant," said

Hermann Sasse. The spirit of the Therian Age—that beast from the earth—is a friendly beast, large and comfortable, warm and fuzzy, welcoming and inclusive, like a great big lovable bear you'd like to hug. In its great arms are enfolded all children of disparate beliefs . . . as long as they love each other. Men and women, gay and straight, find common ground. Protestant and Catholic, Muslim and Jew, liberal and conservative—all are welcome. Love encompasses all.

This beast has teeth and claws, of course. But they stay concealed for the sake of love and inclusiveness. What makes the beast growl and bare its fangs is harshness and intolerance—the kind Elijah showed to Jezebel, Jesus to the Pharisees, Paul to the Judaizers, Augustine to Pelagius, Athanasius to the Arians, Luther to the pope. The kind of intolerance that truth always shows toward error makes the beast very angry. All heretics, when confronted, cry, "Where's the love?" But hardheaded prophets persist, even against brotherly admonition. The beast from the earth has teeth and claws, and they are red with the blood of martyrs.

At the beginning of the New Testament era, Jesus described the Church Militant in terms of offense: "The gates of Hades will not overcome it" (Matthew 16:18). The image is that of an enemy under siege, surrounded and holed up in a walled city, bursting out through the gates from time to time for an incursion, but being driven back in by a superior force. At the end, by contrast, St. John describes the Church Militant in terms of defense: "Satan will be released from his prison and will go out to deceive the nations . . . to gather them for battle. . . . They marched across the breadth of the earth and surrounded the camp of God's people, the city he loves" (Revelation 20:7-9). The image here is of a Church that is oppressed and weary, under long siege, with supplies running short, facing superior numbers, and hanging on determinedly in the hope that rescue will come in time. Perhaps this image of the Church under duress describes our situation today. We may feel like Constantinople under siege by the Turks. We have a good system of ancient bulwarks built by our fathers, but we lack the troops and the discipline to man them. Our God is a mighty fortress; His Church is not.

These realities should not deflect our vision from the hope that is ours in Christ. Things are in disarray ecclesiastically, but at the same time Christ is daily working in this raggedy Church of His. People get saved every day, even through the most mediocre preaching. Souls are sealed for eternity week by week at the most unimpressive baptismal fonts. The feeblest prayers are heard in heaven and answered by a merciful God. People somehow persist in their faith against all odds and despite all setbacks and failures. Little congregations carry on and keep their doors open, nobody quite knows how. The ministry—once a high-prestige, low-stress occupation—is today a high-stress, low-prestige calling in human terms; yet somehow men keep answering the call. Persecution is increasing around the globe; yet Christianity—not Islam—is the fastest-growing religion in the world. False doctrine seeps in everywhere; yet the lamp of God's pure revelation is never completely extinguished.

Meanwhile, just as the devil's church from time to time broke out through its city gates even though surrounded, there is nothing to prevent the Church of Jesus Christ under siege from breaking out and taking captives. Why shouldn't we be aggressive, refusing to stay put behind the barricades? Why shouldn't we show some fighting spirit? Why shouldn't we mount up and ride?

There is something warmly eschatological about the recent animated film *Chicken Run* (indeed, there is something eschatological about a lot of films these days). Ginger, the brave little hen (reprising Steve McQueen in *The Great Escape*), keeps trying to break out of the concentration camp/chicken coop. The other hens are dispirited and defeated, but Ginger keeps trying, the lone visionary against impossible odds. Then a savior comes down from above to help them—in this case a cocky American circus rooster shot from a cannon. There is a final conflict between good and evil—hilarious, like the climax of every good divine comedy. In the end the chickens all fly away to paradise: a bird sanctuary. Somehow I am encouraged by this to fight on. Besides, a study of history makes one notice that the times in which the Church has been the hardest-pressed have also been the times of the greatest missionary activity.

Whether this Therian Age we are entering signals the last of the last days, the end of the end times, no one can say. Only God knows. This world may stumble along for another thousand years. That's only a day to the Lord, anyway. In our pain we are desperate for the relief that will come with Christ's return. But if He delays, we know it is because in His great love and divine mercy there remain a few more souls that can be saved—perhaps through your testimony. As we labor in the vineyard we see the sun that rose in the east now declining in the west. The hour is hastening on. The night comes, when no man can work. We are not in darkness. The appearing of the Lord will delight but not surprise us. We've been expecting Him. We are ready. Others may sleep in carnal security, but we keep our wicks trimmed, our lamps burning, alert, self-controlled, abounding in good works, encouraging one another and building each other up in the most holy faith, and fighting the good fight.

Of course rescue will come in time. The camp of God's people was surrounded by its enemies, "but fire came down from heaven, and devoured them" (Revelation 20:9). Just when it seems that all is lost for the Church under siege, there comes a shout and the sound of a trumpet, lightning flashes from the east to the west, the sign of the cross appears in the sky, and Jesus Christ returns to bring a close to history.

I heard a loud voice from the throne saying, "Now the dwelling of God is with men, and he will live with them. They will be his people, and God himself will be with them and be their God. He will wipe every tear from their eyes. There will be no more death or mourning or crying or pain, for the old order of things has passed away."

—REVELATION 21:3-4

Works Cited

Abel, David. "Paganism Attracts Followers on College Campuses." *Milwaukee Journal Sentinel*. November 12, 2000.

Abrams, M. H., ed. *The Norton Anthology of English Literature*. 2 vols. Sixth edition. New York: Norton, 1993.

Ault, Norman, ed. *Seventeenth Century Lyrics from the Original Texts*. London: Longmans, 1928.

Baym, Nina, ed. *The Norton Anthology of American Literature*. Shorter fifth edition. New York: Norton, 1999.

Bloom, Harold, and David Lehman, eds. *The Best of the Best of American Poetry, 1988-1997*. New York: Scribner, 1998.

Brown, Harold O. J. *The Sensate Culture*. Dallas: Word, 1996.

Cairns, Scott. "The State of the Arts." *Image*. No. 22. Winter/Spring, 1999.

Colson, Charles. "A New Millennium, A New Hope." *Jubilee*. Spring, 1999, p. 19.

——. "Christianity and Women—2000 Years of Jesus." *Breakpoint Commentary*. April 7, 1999.

Dante Alighieri. *The Divine Comedy*. Trans. Charles Eliot Norton. Chicago: Great Books, 1952.

Evans, G. Blakemore, ed. *The Riverside Shakespeare*. Boston: Houghton Mifflin, 1974.

Ferguson, Marilyn. *The Aquarian Conspiracy*. Los Angeles: J. P. Tarcher, 1980.

Griffiths, Bede. *The Golden String*. Springfield, IL: Templegate, 1980.

Hoerber, Robert G., ed. *The Concordia Self-Study Bible* (CSSB). St. Louis: CPH, 1986.

Homer. *The Iliad of Homer and The Odyssey*. Trans. Samuel Butler. Chicago: Great Books, 1952.

Johnston, Barry V. *Pitirim A. Sorokin: An Intellectual Biography*. Lawrence, KS: University of Kansas Press, 1995.

Küng, Hans. *That the World May Believe*. London and New York: Sheed and Ward, 1962.

Lentz, Robert. See http://www.natural-bridges.com.

Lewis, C. S. *God in the Dock: Essays on Theology and Ethics*. Grand Rapids, MI: Eerdmans, 1972.

Lueker, Erwin L., ed. *Lutheran Cyclopedia, Revised Edition* (LC). St. Louis: CPH, 1975.

Lutheran Worship (LW). St. Louis: CPH, 1982.

Martens, Gottfried. "Where Rhine and Tiber Met," in John R. Stephenson and Thomas M. Winger, eds., *Hermann Sasse: A Man for Our Times?* St. Louis: CPH, 1998.

Marx, Karl, and Friedrich Engels. *The Manifesto of the Communist Party*. Trans. Samuel Moore. Chicago: Great Books, 1952.

McElveen, Kelly. "Goddess Worship on the Rise." June 15, 1999. http://www.cbn.org/newsstand/stories/990615.asp

Merton, Thomas. *The Way of Chuang Tzu*. New York: New Directions, 1969.

Miller, Roland E. *Muslim Friends: Their Faith and Feeling*. St. Louis: CPH, 1998.

Pieper, Francis. *Dogmatics*. St. Louis: CPH, 1922. Vol. 3 treats the subject of eschatology.

Sasse, Hermann. *The Lonely Way: Essays and Letters*. Trans. Matthew Harrison. St. Louis: CPH, 2001.

Schmidt, Alvin J. *Under the Influence*. Grand Rapids, MI: Zondervan, 2001.

Sieman-Netto, Uwe. "Faith: Apocalypse Now?" June 6, 2001. http://www.vny.com/cf/news/upidetail.cfm?QID=191965

Sorokin, Pitirim A. *The Crisis of Our Age*. New York: Dutton, 1941.

———. *Social and Cultural Dynamics* (SCD). 4 vols. New York: American Book Co., 1937.

Spengler, Oswald. *The Decline of the West*. Abridg. Helmut Werner. Trans. Charles Francis Atkinson. New York: Modern Library, 1965. Originally published as *Der Untergang des Abendlandes*. Munich: C. H. Beck'sche Verlag, 1918, 1922.

Stephenson, John R. *Eschatology*. In Preus, Robert, ed., *Confessional Lutheran Dogmatics*. Vol. XIII. Dearborn, MI: The Luther Academy, 1993.

Tappert, Theodore, et al. trans. and eds. *The Book of Concord*. Philadelphia: Muhlenberg, 1959.

Toynbee, Arnold J. *Change and Habit: The Challenge of Our Time*. New York and London: Oxford University Press, 1966.

Untermeyer, Louis, ed. *A Treasury of Great Poems, English and American*. New York: Simon & Schuster, 1942.

Virgil. *The Eclogues, The Georgics, The Aeneid*. Chicago: Great Books, 1952.

Wells, H. G. *The Outline of History*. 4 vols. Fourth edition. New York: Collier, 1922.

The World Book Encyclopedia. Chicago: World Book, Inc., 1987.

Index